C000172053

Advanced Introduction to the Cr

Elgar Advanced Introductions are stimulating and thoughtful introductions to major fields in the social sciences and law, expertly written by the world's leading scholars. Designed to be accessible yet rigorous, they offer concise and lucid surveys of the substantive and policy issues associated with discrete subject areas.

The aims of the series are twofold: to pinpoint essential principles of a particular field, and to offer insights that stimulate critical thinking. By distilling the vast and often technical corpus of information on the subject into a concise and meaningful form, the books serve as accessible introductions for undergraduate and graduate students coming to the subject for the first time. Importantly, they also develop well-informed, nuanced critiques of the field that will challenge and extend the understanding of advanced students, scholars and policy-makers.

For a full list of titles in the series please see the back of the book. Recent titles in the series include:

Freedom of Expression
Mark Tushnet

Private Law
Jan M. Smits

Globalisation
Jonathan Michie

Behavioral Economics
John F. Tomer

Environmental Impact Assessment
Angus Morrison-Saunders

National Innovation Systems
Cristina Chaminade, Bengt-Åke Lundvall and Shagufta Haneef

Private International Law and Procedure
Peter Hay

Law and Globalisation
Jaakko Husa

Regional Innovation Systems
Bjørn T. Asheim, Arne Isaksen and Michaela Trippl

International Political Economy
Second Edition
Benjamin J. Cohen

International Tax Law
Second Edition
Reuven S. Avi-Yonah

Social Innovation
Frank Moulaert and Diana MacCallum

The Creative City
Charles Landry

Advanced Introduction to

the Creative City

CHARLES LANDRY

Independent Advisor to Cities

Elgar Advanced Introductions

Cheltenham, UK • Northampton, MA, USA

Published by
Edward Elgar Publishing Limited
The Lypiatts
15 Lansdown Road
Cheltenham
Glos GL50 2JA
UK

Edward Elgar Publishing, Inc.
William Pratt House
9 Dewey Court
Northampton
Massachusetts 01060
USA

A catalogue record for this book
is available from the British Library

Library of Congress Control Number: 2019951071

ISBN 978 1 78897 347 2 (cased)
ISBN 978 1 78897 349 6 (paperback)
ISBN 978 1 78897 348 9 (eBook)

Typeset by Servis Filmsetting Ltd, Stockport, Cheshire
Printed and bound in Great Britain by TJ International Ltd, Padstow

Contents

1   Setting the scene

All humans must be somewhat creative. It is an inbuilt part of our survival instinct. It allows us to cope with the world and adapt to changing circumstances. Yet we have the potential to be even more inventive than we are and we need to be. We say children are creative, and that is inevitable as they must explore the world to imagine how things work and to know what does work. The question is can we maintain this childlike fresh openness and playfulness to ask 'why', 'how' and 'what if' as we age, and in solving the daunting challenges cities face? Can we too create organizational cultures which remain focused and at the same time are willing to reassess what the organization is doing and how?

Talking about individuals and organizations is easier than discussing how a city might become creative. This is a different order of magnitude. It is the theme we explore here.

The book starts stenographically, summarizing in a simple overview the key issues and elements we need to consider in creative city making. Then, rather than providing a straightforward chronological account, it begins by describing what creative and uncreative places are like, reminding us that creativity is present in, and can emerge from, any source – the disenfranchised as well as those with advantages. Following this, the book describes the waves of change that initiated the emergence of creative city thinking.

Then, as someone who tried to shape the creative city idea, the book goes personal. Inevitably our life story fashions how we think and what we do. We are never as objective as we might like to be. So this account is also subjective.

A trajectory of the origins and subsequent developments of creative city making follows, focusing on how a cultural perspective was significant in shaping the ideas. The argument made is that the culture of a people and place determines the scope and possibilities to be creative. Places that are inward-looking differ from those that look outwards.

Next, the book unscrambles the complexities of a city and what creativity is, its qualities and the mindsets required. It stresses, throughout, that creativity needs a purpose and should be driven by ethical concerns. The creative repertoire used by cities worldwide is described, and so we explore cultural resources and planning, creative quarters, districts and zones and propose a way of seeing the city as an asset system. These are a city's raw materials and ingredients.

We look at emergent thinking affecting the creativity of cities, and especially psychological dimensions, as well as the impacts of digitization – a game changer. The book closes by proposing how you can measure and evaluate the creativity of a city.

Words and concepts go in and out of fashion, but at the core of the creative city is the notion that imagination and inventiveness are crucial in keeping a city alive, alert, adaptable and relevant to the problems that matter in the world today as it is buffeted by the winds of change. This will not change, and in this sense the concept is trend resistant.

It is important to remember that creative places have existed throughout history. Athens gave us an intellectual heritage that fostered debate, analysis and critique, which in its then very old context was somewhat progressive, even though women had few rights and slavery as in other societies. Venice highlights to us the importance of specialization, expertise and trade networks in its astonishing rise to control most of the Mediterranean. Florence and Siena remind us how important new business models are, such as the invention of accounting and banking systems. The rise of Paris as an arts, fashion and gastronomy leader in the 19th century shows how royal extravagance can inspire more popular expressions of culture. Vienna shows us how a configuration of core ideas in psychology, the arts and literature can affect a number of disciplines simultaneously. London of the swinging 60s hit a global mood of change whereby the young wanted to challenge existing hierarchies and ways of thinking, and the success of Silicon Valley helps point out the elements required – organizational, financial and legal – to turn ideas into reality. Here the role of university research and its link to venture capital was key.

Interestingly, as an aside, caffeine and coffee houses were important in most of these movements as social hubs for intellectuals and artists to meet and as centres for political discussion and making commercial deals. Kiva Han, established in 1555 in Constantinople/Istanbul, was reputedly the first. They remain important today as third places, neither home nor an office, to work and to socialize, often with more formal co-working spaces attached.

Today, especially in Europe, the participative imperative is rising up the agenda, so contemporary urban creativity will have a different focus. That notion, though, is contested globally. The kinds of empowerment agendas or civic activism common, say, in Nordic countries are perceived as a threat in China, Russia or authoritarian states. Thus, developing new forms of civic engagement or reinventing democratic processes can be creative, as, by contrast, can be the ability to subvert regimes to get your voice heard. The Extinction Rebellion, which is focused on the urgency of addressing climate change, stresses that at times mass civil disobedience can be a catalyst. Their chant 'Dear police we love you, we're doing this for our children' made many of the police cry. The same applies to Greta Thunberg's 'school strike for climate' campaign or Polly Higgins' long-term attempt to make ecocide – the deliberate destruction of the natural environment – a crime against humanity. This is a form of legal creativity and could be a game changer and force business to operate differently, especially given the chorus of voices from the United Nations (UN) downwards that we face a systemic crisis and a business-as-usual approach will not solve the problems we face.

These all involve different forms of imagination. The same applies to other big issues such as rising inequality or establishing a green economy, which require us to bend and contain market forces and direct them to bigger-picture purposes.

Today we can discuss creativity being applied to any field, but back in the late 1980s when most of the constituent ideas were developed, the key terms discussed were culture, the arts, cultural planning, cultural resources, cultural literacy and the cultural industries, as those were then seen as the crucial issues to address at that time.

The original focus on creativity began as people started to recognize – especially in Britain, and then the United States and Europe – that:

- Dramatic structural changes were afoot whereby many cities began to weaken economically as industry moved to the East. Cities then asked themselves 'who are we now' and began to find in their culture a source of strength that could help in the remaking.
- A new economy was emerging within which design, the audio-visual and new digitally driven sectors, and performance and events would become much more important.
- The promise of globalization was diversity and distinctiveness but sadly the result was sameness. The urban environment was becoming homogeneous, standardized, dull and dispiriting as the construction and development industries were beginning to have ever-greater power in determining how cities evolved and looked, as were the corporations, with similar shops and environments being built all over the world.
- The old fabric of the city was being thoughtlessly destroyed in the name of urban renewal without considering the value of the old and how this could be blended with the new.
- Cultural experiences were being made into commodities as globalization was making every place look and feel the same with similar brand names dominating everything. Local distinctiveness was declining and eroding.
- Artists were increasingly being seen as having a strong role in helping to explore place identity and distinctiveness and that this could have a positive impact for cities.

Two big issues are significant. First, it is the self-conscious and planned approach to establishing 'creative places' that is new. This immediately raises a dilemma as to the extent to which you can plan 'creativity'. All that can happen from a planning perspective is to generate the enabling conditions, both physical and in terms of activities for people and organizations to act imaginatively. These conditions sometimes involve a public authority creating new regulations to support more sustainable development, providing cheap space or grant systems to help support businesses, loosening planning regulations to hold events in unusual places, or encouraging temporary uses in areas waiting for development.

Periods of history involving mass transformation – like the Industrial Revolution, or the technological revolution of the past 50 years – can produce confusion, a sense of liberation combined with a feeling of being swept along by events. It thus takes a while for new ethical stances to take root or to establish a new and coherent worldview. Crucially, in such times of powerful transformation when cities moved from one phase or economy to the next, every city needed to ask itself 'what is my role and purpose?', 'what human, cultural and physical resources do I have which I can draw on?' and 'what is the best way of managing and organizing my city to be effective?' This led to soul searching, and many cities around the world concluded that the old way of doing things did not work sufficiently well:

- Education did not seem to prepare students and adults for the demands of the 'new' world.
- Organization, management and leadership in both the private and the public sectors, with its control ethos and hierarchical focus, did not provide the flexibility, adaptability and resilience to cope with the increasingly intense competitive global environment, nor with the rising demands by citizens who wanted a greater say in decision making.
- City planning, in dealing with the industrial legacy, was insufficiently able to understand how to make a city attractive, liveable for locals but also rich in opportunities. By being more competitive and thus wealth creating, its most gifted people would be more likely to stay, while outsiders and investors would be attracted to come.
- The development industry was underperforming and was therefore urged to 'up its game' and to move on from a 'down to a price' approach to one based on 'up to a standard'. Here aesthetics became more important.

2 Highlights and summary

- The creative city notion connects the triad creativity, culture and the city together in exploring how places navigate the waves of urban transformation.
- There is a need to switch the question: not 'what is the value of imagination and creativity for city development?' but instead 'what is the cost of not thinking of imagination and creativity?' Name a city that is compelling, resilient, sustainable, attractive and important, but has weak ambition and imagination.
- The creative city looks at the immense problems we face from a 'glass half full' approach. It always asks 'can this problem be addressed in a fresh way?' or 'is this problem an opportunity in disguise?' It was and is a response to the dramatic transformations cities face.
- The agendas of creative city making have changed since their origins in the late 1980s. The priorities of the 2020s are different. The initial cultural focus remains significant. Only by understanding the history, the culture, the DNA and assets of a place can we assess its potential. Yet the emphasis of creative action should shift with the times to address our current urgent problems and opportunities. Fostering the UN's Sustainable Development Goals is one such need.
- The 'creative city making' concept seeks to create a shift in paradigm. It seeks to harness the collective imagination of a place and create the conditions for people, organizations and the city as a whole to think, plan and act with imagination in fostering opportunities and in solving day-to-day and exceptional problems in a fresh way.
- The central assumption is that ordinary people can make the extraordinary happen if given the chance. This focus on empowerment can generate the confidence for people to get engaged and to act.
- It is a clarion call to think differently and highlights a particular way of thinking and a differing map for organizing and managing

cities. It describes a new wider world of thought and worldview for planning and urban development disciplines. This can highlight or uncover hidden resources – some tangible and others intangible, and many coming from the deeper history of a place.

- The creative city idea advocates the need for a culture of creativity to be embedded into how the urban stakeholders operate. By encouraging and legitimizing the use of imagination in all spheres, the 'ideas bank' of possibilities and potential solutions broadens. This is the divergent thinking that generates multiple options and ideas. It needs to be aligned to convergent thinking that narrows down possibilities and sorts out the good ideas from the bad. This is called 'going through the reality checker'.

- Urban creativity needs a purpose, an aim and an ethical frame. This includes giving back to its community and even to the world. It is better to be the most creative city for the world rather than in the world. The aim is to help a city region to become more resilient, to future-proof itself, to be more socially responsible, to become more prosperous and to enhance the well-being of citizens.

- By being strategically principled and tactically flexible it is possible to ensure that the higher goals of a creative city agenda are not side tracked. Those principles ensure that one has strong guidelines for action whilst maintaining the fluidity necessary to adapt to changing circumstances.

- This ethical framework and moral compass should guide a city's imaginative energies and actions. The dynamic of our current economic system is 'materially expansive, socially divisive and environmentally hostile'.[1] Today a deep concern to be sustainable in every sense is one such priority. Another is to develop a human-centred, human scale or humane environment where people's needs are primary. A third is to ensure people drive technology rather than the reverse, or to develop a rich, multilayered experience for those living in a city.

- A special ethos is required to be self-consciously innovative across a broad front from technology to social innovation. To embed this ethos, from ecological building to powerful public art, within often economically or culturally conservative structures is difficult.

- All through history the city has been the hub for transactions and exchange: of ideas, of knowledge, of trade, of services and

---

1 https://ec.europa.eu/info/sites/info/files/research_and_innovation/research_by_area/documents/ec_rtd_decarbonisation-report_112018.pdf.

potentially of creative possibilities. The city was ever the place where mixing and interacting happened in spite of separations between classes, groups, the rich and the poor, the powerful and the disenfranchised.

- This highlights the diversity agenda in all its forms. Being positive about diversity can enrich. All of this requires a vast number of new perspectives or innovations. Acknowledging this potential is a matter of politics.

- The city has always been a source of problems as well as a laboratory for finding inventive solutions to any problems it creates. Now the primary focus should be on creating innovations to heal the environmental distress in cities, and second to find ways that the diversity of people in cities can coexist in better harmony and to encourage a 360-degree holistic perspective to ensure the complexity of the city is fully understood.

- Creativity was invariably a key attribute in city making. The difference between the past and today is that cities are now self-consciously encouraging and planning to create the enabling preconditions for creativity. Its central characteristic is to foster a more open mindset, management style and organizational structure for inventive ideas and projects to flourish. This allows a city to respond to changing circumstances and to become adaptable.

- Creativity is context driven. What was 'creative' in the 19th or 20th century will be different from what is creative in the 21st. What is regarded as creative in one culture and in one circumstance will differ in another. However, there are principles of creativity that cut across all cultures and time. These include a combination of openness and childlike freshness, along with the ability to connect the seemingly disconnected and to see patterns across different issues.

- Making the most of a city implies an integrated mindset and operating style. It acknowledges the specific sub-sector perspectives and knowledge, but stresses that silo thinking has limitations. It highlights a deeper understanding of cultural dynamics and drivers as well as social needs, along with a focus on 'what really matters' for our cities – now. This has implications for the priorities a city sets itself. Ultimately it changes the feel of the city and the ways it goes about its city-making business.

- The idea of civic creativity I developed in 1998 is crucial. This is defined as imaginative problem solving applied to public good and public interest objectives. It seeks to combine an entrepreneurial attitude while maintaining the focus on issues of equity and transparency. 'Civic creativity' is the capacity for public officials, businesses (large and small) or civil society organizations to together generate a flow of opportunities to improve urban life.

- A creative person can be a scientist, an artist, a businessperson, a social activist, a bureaucrat, an urban planner, a politician or an ordinary citizen. It is their personal attributes that make them creative. However, creativity is legitimized in some spheres more than others.

- Being creative is a way of thinking, with openness its key attribute. Other characteristics include curiosity; a questioning attitude; the ability to stand back, listen and reassess; the courage not to take a given credo, practice or theory for granted and to dare to think outside of the conventional; and the gift of seeing relevance and connections between apparently different things. This applies to individuals, organizations and the city itself.

- Creativity becomes a flexible, multifaceted resource with its qualities shaping people's mindset. This affects the culture of the city. Not every person or place is equally creative, but everywhere can become more creative than it already is.

- Imaginative thinking has wide significance cutting across all forms of knowledge including science, technology and the arts, with applications in the social, political and economic domains and all industries.

- The skills and insights needed to develop good, imaginative, self-sustaining cities need to combine cultural, social, psychological, anthropological, technological and economic knowledge as well as 'creativity' whose essence is a multifaceted resourcefulness. It is a primary asset since human cleverness, desires, motivations and imagination are replacing location, natural resources and market access as key urban resources.

- Creativity can come from any source, and often the inventive solutions found by or linked to the poor are undervalued. Microfinance initiated in India is an example.

- An innovation in one context may be ordinary in another. Turning an old industrial building into a creative economy incubator may be common practice in Europe but a novelty elsewhere. Or developing a city vision through a public–private and civic growth alliance may happen frequently in Europe or North America but rarely elsewhere.

- There is an important distinction between creativity and innovation. The journey has a trajectory starting with encouraging people in your city to be curious. If they are curious, then they can become imaginative. With imagination it is possible to conceive and reconceive things and to envision possible futures. Then it is possible to be creative and to have ideas. These in turn need to go through the reality checker and to be tested. Only some of the creative ideas will survive and become an invention. Once widely applied they become an innovation.

- Creativity on its own is not enough. It only gains true importance when an idea is turned into an applied innovation and reality and is allied to other qualities such as motivation, tenacity, awareness, clarity of communication, broad thinking, inspiration, adaptability, dynamism, openness, sensory appreciation, professional pride and technical competence, leadership or vision.
- Being creative or innovative for its own sake can be harmful. Sometimes the creative act is to leave things as they are. Old ideas are not always useless, yet our current growth-driven economy inexorably impels us to innovate to keep the system going.
- City making is one of the most important human endeavours since it deals with the conditions for people and groups to live together in relative harmony, both with each other and with nature. The latter is crucial given the dramatic implications of climate change, so it must be a central focus of any future creativity initiative.
- Planning as we know it is still largely focused on the physical aspects, urban design and architecture, important as they are. It is seen from the air and mostly driven by a top-down approach, but there is much more to city planning.
- The rise of the 'right to the city movement' sees more people for more reasons wanting involvement so they can become shapers, makers and co-creators of their evolving city. Rights, though, need to be linked to responsibilities, and to make that real it needs a good operating context.
- There is a paradox: the more we discuss creativity the more the world has adopted a culture of risk aversion. The evaluation of everything from a perspective of risk has become a defining characteristic of contemporary society.
- The attributes and attitudes that made building our cities seemingly successful in the last 50 years may hinder their potential in achieving their aims to create great liveable cities in the future. That path dependency is dangerous. One thinks here of many hardware infrastructures, such as road systems and car dependency. Those ideas are now being challenged.
- There is an older and newer thinking about cities in relation to planning and design, organization and management, the use of

resources, the role of culture and how cities project themselves. The new planning paradigm should supersede the previously dominant model of urban development focused on the hardware of the city. I call this the 'culture of engineering' approach.

- The world of cities is changing dramatically. Notions of what makes great places and cities changes as well as ideas of what we should do and who should be responsible for planning them, so new agendas are coming to the fore. There are urgent questions that we all face. These include the immense impacts of digitization with its positive opportunities but also its negative impacts, the challenges of diversity, or the increased dangers of climate change.

- The nomadic world is changing the nature of belonging, identity and where we are anchored as we can now operate anywhere and anytime. Where, then, are the zones of encounter, and how do we create places of empathy between insiders and outsiders? This new world is enabled by digitization.

- Successful creative city making understands urbanity. This is the art and science of how the hardware and the software of a city blend together and how a good physical fabric can help generate a multifaceted inclusive vitality. This involves a new understanding of what urban assets are, new ways of working to maximize potential and new competences.

- A city is not a set of lifeless buildings and roads, but primarily the activities of people who bring it to life. This means integrated teams comprising those with knowledge of people, social and economic dynamics and culture need to work with those who understand transport, engineering, physical planning, recreation and housing issues. The agendas, strategies and plans are best when they are jointly conceived, planned and implemented.

- The cities we have mostly disappoint. More of them are ugly rather than beautiful. Few reflect truly the diversities that make up most urban populations. Most are unsustainable. Most look the same with their large tower blocks, often with suburbs sprawling endlessly into the far horizon. There is too much traffic and noise. A few places delight.

- At the origin of the creative city idea in the late 1980s people tended to think it was concerned mostly with artists and the creative economy sectors like design, new media, music, film or performing arts as well as the associated cultural infrastructure like museums or galleries. That view on its own is too limited: they are not the exclusive realm of creativity, yet they can play a significant role in fostering the creative urban agenda. Their impacts are strong. The best cultural policies combine a focus on enlightenment, empowerment, entertainment, employability and creating economic impact.

- The notion of cultural resources was central in creative city making. These were the raw materials of a city, its assets, its cultural attitudes and its value base. These then were typically mapped, on the basis of which cultural planning and strategy making can take place. Additionally an understanding of cultural literacy is important, which is the knowledge of how people with differing cultural backgrounds think and act.

- Retrospectively, colleagues and I made a mistake. Instead of saying 'cultural planning' it should have been 'planning culturally'. The first implies too much that it is about the arts or cultural infrastructures, whereas the latter concept signifies a deeper understanding of culture and its drivers in planning anything.

- Additionally, defining the 'creative economy' as a series of narrow sectors is ultimately unhelpful as the task is to encourage 'creativity in the economy' as a whole, and equally legitimize the creativity of others such as interesting bureaucrats.

- Cheap space is crucial. Urban areas, especially the light industrial belt surrounding many city centres whose industrial purposes had declined, became attractive to artists given their large spaces and cheap rent. Using the arts consciously as a trigger to regenerate became part of the urban regeneration repertoire and city strategies. Artists catalysed the notion of adaptive reuse.

- This process initiated the long wave of revaluing heritage by blending arts, creative economy activities and ultimately the wider start-up culture and especially high-tech business.

- There have been critiques of the creative city idea claiming it is only targeted at hipsters, property developers and those who gentrify areas or seek to glamorize them so destroying local distinctiveness. This has happened in places, but it is not inevitable. Those groups may have used and abused the term, but this was not the intention of the notion in its origins. Remember, the notion always stressed the importance of ethics. The creative challenge is to find appropriate regulations and incentives to obviate the negative aspects.

- A special and valid concern has been the conscious use of artists to be the vanguard of gentrification, to lift property values and to make areas safe before others move in. This is called artwashing.

- The creative city notion is in danger of hollowing out by general overuse of the word 'creative' as applied to people, activities, organizations, urban neighbourhoods or cities that objectively are not especially creative.

- A similar process has happened with other monikers that became popular after the 'creative city' idea, such as 'knowledge city', 'innovative city', 'green city' and 'smart city'. Concepts are being used like consumables – use them, digest them, then find and popularize a new term. It is difficult to find trend-resistant terms.
- Digitization is a merger between computing power and the Internet, and is a game changer. It is an animating force and has created a completely new environment. This changes the context within which we discuss creativity in cities. The interactive possibilities of social media make new trajectories of inclusion and exclusion possible.
- An under-explored dimension is the 'creative bureaucracy' which is gaining traction across the globe. It has three pillars: reassessing the rules and incentives regime, rethinking the inner life of the bureaucracy to enable people to give of their best, and finding new ways of connecting with citizens and organizations in a digitizing world.
- In a creative city there will be a portfolio of innovative actions – an urban innovation ecosystem. Some will be real shifts in inventiveness, such as reconceiving waste as a resource or seeing the city as an 'urban commons' jointly managed by citizens and the authorities. Others will be good practices most places now follow. Think here of valuing heritage as an asset rather than a cost, or seeing cultural activities as a driver for economic growth, or shifting mobility from car dominance to other modes like public transport, cycling or micro-scooters. Once, those ideas were seen as very innovative.
- Today a central driver and engine for city development is its ability to keep and to attract highly skilled, ambitious, talented and imaginative people to the city. This is an investment in future prosperity. Crucially, such people, who have choices about where to live, increasingly choose the city before the company or job. This means a city needs to rethink its look, feel, appeal and atmosphere to entice these potentially interesting people.
- Secondary, smaller or shrinking cities should now become the focus for creative action as they suffer from the vortex effect of very successful cities that, like a vacuum cleaner, suck up the ambitious, the money and the opportunities.
- Not everyone is highly ambitious or expert. A good city takes those people equally seriously as each person can make a contribution as

an active citizen. It is the rich civic life of a city that is a significant factor of urban success.

- Liveability, which is the ability to create good facilities, to foster distinctiveness or to value people's needs and desires, moves centre stage in addressing urban development. The agendas of knowledge nomads and local people often align on liveability issues, such as good connectivity or the desire to highlight the uniqueness of a place. Yet the wish to be exploratory, which is important to pioneering people, is less of an issue for most citizens.

- Creativity is a powerful, soft resource with a set of attributes that can help the lifeblood of a place and its distinctiveness and add value. It can, for instance, enhance products, services, processes and techniques as well as how the city itself is shaped and develops.

- Creativity is now seen as a new currency, the equivalent to having finance capital. It is equally important. There are also others forms of capital that together can make better cities, including human, social, heritage, knowledge and leadership capital. Capital here is understood as potential or energy.

- By thinking imaginatively, many new resources and possibilities are uncovered. It is the 21st-century version of natural resources. We have moved from a world where natural advantages determined potential to one where harnessing and mobilizing creative advantage more effectively than others determines a city's success.

- By creating the conditions for people to think, work and act with imagination, a creative milieu is established. It is both a physical setting and a set of activities and attitudes that shape the way the city operates. This gives the city its personality. Within this, specific sectors may be creative, such as a specialism like the shoe or machinery industry, or the arts or information technology (IT). These alone are insufficient to be deemed a creative city as that is more than just having some creative projects in a city.

- To establish a self-reinforcing virtuous cycle of creativity you need a critical mass of differing activities that explore new possibilities and solutions to problems. There are few lone heroes/heroines. Mostly we achieve together and through collaboration.

- Bringing together varied disciplines and interesting couplings – be that scientists and artists, tech- and craft-focused people, or those in Impact Hub networks with their social priorities and progressive businesses – can create a rich seam of solutions

- This clustering process is helped by initiatives such as co-working or incubator spaces, that cater to people and organizations at differing levels of development.

- It is very unusual for a city to be comprehensively creative, stretching across all economic sectors to new forms of housing or social affairs. Many cities have attempted to create innovative quarters or districts, often focused on one dimension such as new technology, a special sector like the automotive or space industries, or the creative economy. Rarely are such districts built around social innovations.

- A truly creative place has a *'creative ecology'*, where all the interconnected systems that make a city function are open to being reassessed when necessary. Being creative does not mean everything needs to be reinvented. There is, though, a willingness to look at things afresh, after which some things will be deemed to need changing and others not. This may involve transport systems, systems dealing with social affairs, systems developing new business ideas, or even systems managing the city itself.

- A city does not reach an end point when it is then creative. The concept is dynamic not static; it is more a process than a plan. There is a need to be constantly alert in assessing opportunities. A creative city is a place that is evolving.

- This means being willing to review the tried and tested and to be able to assess well when to open out possibilities and when to close in and be focused.

- Creating an industrial city, which is hardware focused and where a 'culture of engineering' dominates, is a different process from creative city making with its concern for both the software and the hardware of the city.

- The software of the city includes focusing on its civic life, its culture, its formal and informal learning systems, the way people across organizations can network, interact and meet, or the atmosphere generated within the city through activities and facilities.

- The city can feel opaque and obscure. It is difficult to see the city in its totality both from within and how it expresses itself externally. We mostly see its external appearance. Rarely do we detect the creative energy often hidden behind walls. Therefore, many things stand as a proxy or substitute indicating its creativity. This might be its cultural vitality, its events, its gastronomy and cafés, or its unusual buildings, the streetscape or its facilities.

- A city should not simplistically claim it is a creative city. Perhaps it might call itself an 'emerging creative city' as a sign of its aspirations, but preferably it should be others who call your city creative. Here there are elements of push and pull. You push through your intentions and through creative achievements a virtuous cycle ensues where you are pulled by the external recognition you get.

- We can assess how creative a city is, and there are measures and indicators across domains, but these depend on our priorities. Nowadays, ecological or 'cradle to cradle' thinking, or understanding the bio-economy, is also key, as is cultural literacy – the understanding of how others think.

- Creativity usually challenges the tried and tested, the accepted canon and the existing hierarchy, or holding onto tradition. There can be a tense equilibrium, often balancing the old and the new. Creative places can be uncomfortable. There is a creative rub. To make the most of these places often requires new laws, new regulations or new incentives. Yet in an open-minded place which fosters a culture of discussion and debate, this tension can be productive. It can make the city alive and vital.

- There is a deeper impulse that drives our wish to change, adapt, seek improvements or innovate. It is our need to survive and our innate sense of playfulness as human beings. It is this childlike playfulness that on occasion we need to recapture.

- To conclude: Good creative city making is more like the best of improvised jazz rather than a well-tempered symphony performance.

3   Uncreative and creative places[1]

Not every city is vibrant and energetic or stands at the hub of global affairs. Yet every city has a reason for being, a history and a function. There are more ordinary than extraordinary places fulfilling their role, from being a port to being a market or commuter town. Cities rise and fall over time, and not many keep their relevance over the very long term.

Many cities start with similar assets. They have a good location, they are at the crossroads of trade, they are blessed with natural resources, and they are a centre of power, learning or even a cult. Some make the most of their potential; they are alert and forward focused, building on their resources or, when necessary, adapting to new conditions and reinventing their purpose afresh. Others do not.

Some cities find themselves in a difficulty outside of their control; for example, their resources have run out (cities with a fishing industry), the goods they produce have been priced out of the market due to cheaper foreign competition (steel or textile cities), they are less in fashion now (tourist destinations), or new transport links have bypassed them and shifted centrality (a new railway line or airport hub). For example, the rise of Dubai and Madrid has reduced the position of Bangkok and Barcelona. Cities rise and fall: think of Athens, Jerusalem, Tangiers, Bruges or Liverpool. Those with heritage tend to become tourist destinations, but is that enough? Also think of cities which peaked in the industrial era: Baltimore, Cincinnati and the numerous cities in Eastern Europe. Yet all these could benefit from being inventive and sharp. They could make higher-value goods from steel by moving up the value chain, or redefine their tourism offering, or perhaps create a new niche.

---

1 This chapter draws on Landry and Hyams (2012).

What is an uncreative place like?

There are many uncreative places, and one thing we know is that in time they will fail and decline in spite of any initial intrinsic advantages. Let us imagine these uninspiring places before describing a more ideal creative city.

Many cities unfortunately become complacent, considering only the tried and tested, losing energy and maybe just hoping that luck will come their way. Here existing power structures hold on to their status; they reject ideas or refuse to let new people in. Rather like a company in decline, they do not reassess their business model or think of a new ambition, vision and purpose. They become somewhat obstinate and focus on past achievements. This pride can hold them back. They stick to their – perhaps archaic – rules without checking if they suit the current environment. There is a dominant inward-looking attitude, and fewer connections are made both internally and with the outside world. People, businesses, public bodies and organizations generally work alone, rarely thinking that perhaps a partnership could provide a faster and better route to problem solving – in fact they fear collaboration, seeing it as a threat and a potential for competitors. They are self-referential and less vigilant and alert. They are not aware of the new global agendas, such as the need to develop sustainably, or that car dominance can make their place less liveable. This dampens the entrepreneurial spirit. Over time this becomes a vicious circle. It is difficult to get resources for renewal, and this drains the spirit so that more ambitious or talented people want to leave even if they still have some affection for their place of origin. They have given up hope of meeting their desires. Potential leaks out. The city has less scope to invest in its young and its educational reputation tends to go down. Infrastructures look tired, standards decline, and even the urban environment is not well kept. There is too little life in the atmosphere.

What is a creative place like?

On the other hand, it is perhaps quite inspiring to describe the atmosphere, look and feel of an ideal or imaginary creative place.

A creative place is somewhere where people can express their hopes, talents and potential, which are harnessed, exploited and promoted for the common good. Things get done. These talents act as a catalyst and role model for the development and attraction of further interesting people. It is a place with myriad, high-quality learning opportunities, formal and informal, with a forward-looking and adaptable curriculum. The physical environment functions well for its inhabitants; it is easy to move around and connect with each other. Its high-level urban design inspires, stimulates and generates pride and affection. The architecture, old and new, is well assembled, and the street pattern is diverse and interesting. Webbed within the ordinary is the occasional extraordinary and remarkable. It is an environment in which creators of all kinds are content and motivated to create and where there are outlets and channels to exploit innovations or to sell their work. It is a natural marketplace, where people exchange ideas, develop joint projects, trade their products or work in its advanced industries. They develop many innovations and are aware that these should fit agendas like the UN Sustainable Development Goals. They are environmentally conscious; they try to become carbon neutral and adopt 'cradle to cradle' thinking. They have an ethical outlook and seek to be pioneering in a socially responsible way. They include rather than exclude and try to create opportunities for all.

This place communicates well both internally and to the external world. It offers rich, vibrant experiences through, for example, gastronomy, the arts, heritage and its natural surroundings, including thriving mainstream and alternative scenes and a healthy network of third spaces. Opportunities abound: the place is welcoming and encouraging. Its dynamism makes it a magnet and so generates critical mass that guarantees longevity.

The public sector has clarity in its perspective and direction and understands the importance of harnessing the potential of its people. It is lean, clear and focused. Its workings are easy to navigate, and it is accessible, open and encourages participation. Public employees here are focused on the job at hand regardless of departmental boundaries. Differences are a natural part of this discussion culture. They are debated, accepted, negotiated and resolved without rancour. Its leadership has vision and is strategic yet is grounded in day-to-day reality. It is respected and trusted and recognizes its vital role in continuously identifying new opportunities and future-proofing. The society it governs has a high degree of cohesion and is relatively open to incomers and to new ideas, even though these ideas can sometimes be uncomfortable – indeed, creative places are often not that cosy and can be somewhat edgy. This society enjoys its status as a creative hub and the physical environment in which it exists. Levels of crime are in general low, the place feels safe, and standards of living are relatively high. It is socially alert and seeks to avoid ghettoizing its poorest. Social organizations are active, well-funded and constructive.

Industry is innovative and design aware, with a strong focus on new trends, such as developing the green economy; emerging technologies, such as those arising from digitalization; and fledgling sectors, such as the creative industries. It is well networked and well connected, and its commitment to research and development is well above average. Cross-fertilization across even the most diverse sectors occurs as a matter of course. This process often happens in hubs, incubation centres or specially designated districts, and these are not detached from the rest of the city. The business community is entrepreneurial, has drive and is forward-thinking. It understands and utilizes well its natural resources, and it harnesses existing talents while acting as a breeding ground for new skills and enabling its young to feel wanted. Business leaders are respected figures in their community and give something back. The community in turn is proud of their products and the reputation they bring to the place. Overall the city makes good use of its effective communications systems, including local and international transport, high-speed Internet access and connectivity to the world at large.

You feel that this place has something we might call *civic urbanity*. Being civic is to be a full citizen, where people are engaged with their city in multiple ways on an ongoing basis in order to improve their lives and those of others. It projects a sense that 'me' and 'my city' merge into one. Its urbanity reflects a place that has social mobility, where participation is encouraged and where pride in place is reflected in innumerable ways ranging from generous public gestures to urban design, enlightened institutions, lively activity programmes and support for those less fortunate.

The best of this place comes together in gathering places or civic precincts where public facilities such as a museum, a square or a pavement intermesh with private facilities or shops, but where the overall tone is one of civic generosity – the city giving back to its citizens. These desirable places enable us to experience the moment: a place open for coincidence – rather than having to do something specific and always move on to the next thing.

Overall, as in all creative places, this place is unlike any other. You can feel and sense the buzz, it is obvious to residents and visitors alike. It accentuates its distinctiveness in a relaxed and unthreatening way. It is at ease with itself. Its history, culture and traditions are alive, receptive to influence and change, absorbing new ideas which in turn evolve and develop its distinctiveness and culture.

Reference

Landry, Charles and Jonathan Hyams (2012), *The Creative City Index: Measuring the Pulse of Your City*, Stroud, UK: Comedia.

4   Waves of change

To understand how the creative city agenda evolved we need to see the deeper context from within which it emerged and the long waves of change. A curve shows the movement over time from the agrarian to the creativity or digitally driven economy. We were primarily an agrarian society for millennia, an industrial one for 200 years, then a society whose wealth creation was largely driven by the value created by information for 30 years; we now talk of the knowledge, innovation and digitally driven economies, where big data and smart apps presage worlds of artificial intelligence and where the digitizing world has created a new culture. Here the openness associated with creativity plays a significant role. Crucially too, as automation threatens more and more jobs, those that are safer are ones with strong creative input. All we have left, some say, is creativity.

More speedily, we have moved through phases where the dominance of a particular asset has changed and is highlighted. Another way of expressing this is that our economies and the social life built around them were first factor driven, then efficiency driven, and then innovation driven or creativity driven. Each implies a growing level of complexity.

Each metaphor such as the 'the innovation economy' or 'the creativity-driven economy' provides a helpful lens through which to understand and gauge the shift in the primary means of wealth creation, the life it creates, the basis of competition and collaboration, the social and cultural priorities, the management style and operating systems, the role of the public sector and the measurement of success or failure. Now we have reached a stage where creativity and the capacity to imagine is seen as key as technological determinism narrows our scope to even think 'what could be'.

Every shift in the means of economic wealth creation creates a new social order, new ways of learning and things to learn, new settings in which learning takes place and the demand for new kinds of facilities. It requires different cultural capabilities. For instance, looking at the economy, the capabilities and requirements to set up a Ford Motor Company or a Wal Mart are different from those to create an Apple or a Google, or a Kaos Pilots educational centre in Denmark or a Forum Virium in Helsinki.

The 'innovation or knowledge economy', for instance, is largely associated with technological innovation and the skills, attitudes and qualities of technologists, software engineers and other engineering or scientifically oriented people. Without wishing to stumble into stereotypes, the personality characteristics of these groups tend to be more logical, linear, rational, analytical and systematic, and while of course they have elements of creativity as well, they might be less adept at appreciating social or justice issues, or may lack the ability to communicate well. Surveys, for instance, show that engineers need to pay greater attention to interpersonal skills, communicative abilities and cultural literacy.

There was a level of predictability about the results of the former phases associated with industrialism. Predicting exactly the 'emerging advantages' from creativity is less easy, especially as it is now linked to the digital world. We are moving from a *'managing the known'* world to one, given the uncertainties of climate change impacts and tensions emerging from the dislocations of globalization, of *'building the unknown'*. Yet what is possible is to build capability and resilience, and to encourage the mindset of communities to have foresight. Here, identifying what the 'advantage' might be differs, as other important issues start to emerge, such as a focus on equality. So what are the creative capacities to address these? This requires political will and a governance ethos, as well as an aware management and learning system willing to adapt to these new necessities.

These transitions are not smooth; there are social ruptures and tensions, and there are winners and losers. Cities that claim to be creative often have many poor people living in them, along with ghettoes and disenfranchised people, and are often badly run. So the scope of creativity must be comprehensive and include creative solutions to social issues.

The knowledge-intensive economy

Slowly, and with gathering force from the 1960s onwards, it became clear that Western societies were changing profoundly. Authors such as Fritz Machlup (1962), Peter Drucker (1969), Alain Touraine (1971) and Daniel Bell (1973) discussed the coming of a post-industrial society based less on muscle power and more on brain power and its resulting knowledge. Of course, the industrial era also required knowledge, but the difference with the emerging era was its self-conscious use. A series of interlocking issues and common themes highlighted were that information industries will rise in importance; knowledge is a vital form of capital and an economic resource; science-based industries will drive the economy; new ideas can grow the economy; the evolving economy is information and knowledge led and service oriented, with a shift from manufacturing to services.

The raw materials of this new system are increasingly information, knowledge and creativity. This is the soil from within which ideas about creativity grew. Knowledge here is both a product in itself and a tool to enhance the value of other activities. It is not just the 'ingredients' (supply) that makes good food, it is the 'recipe' (knowledge) that counts too, as Paul Romer noted.[1]

Knowledge is the next level up from information, since through judgement and analysis it adds value to any idea, product or service. The analysis of information in itself can have vast impacts, as the arrival of big data 30 years later revealed in creating a quantum leap in what is possible. Looking back then, what is happening now seemed unimaginable, such as how live information helps the logistics industry or the ability to create just-in-time production processes. Knowledge is essentially human capital and it accentuates the different types of skills and workers needed to run a society. In a more knowledge-intensive economy, the specialized labour force is more maths and computer literate and data savvy. That knowledge entails a variety of subject and technical expertise areas and the intellectual capacity to problem solve and discover opportunities. Companies always seek to inscribe knowledge into their processes and products so that it cannot escape with those who hold it. However, to drive these largely profit-maximizing economic engines requires new ideas and inventions.

---

1 http://www.econlib.org/library/Enc/EconomicGrowth.html.

Knowledge can grow rather than deplete by being shared and applied. This shifts the economy from one of scarcity to potential abundance. Allied to this is the global reach enabled by the digital world and the creation of collective intelligence through connectivity and interactivity and vastly easier access to knowledge sources. A characteristic is the speed of transaction and agility of processes. The dynamic pushing knowledge is that knowledge-enhanced products or services are more expensive than those with low embedded knowledge. Strong communication abilities are vital to make knowledge flow, and this affects social structures and the cultural setting of organizations and cities.

The impacts of the evolving knowledge-intensive economy were dramatic on the organization of work and cities. The deindustrialization process in the West reduced the power of blue-collar workers and their unions with a rise of professional workers and the 'creative' professions associated with design or new media. Regretfully there are always winners and losers in these dramatic transformations. So as the need to encourage creativity came, the essential question remained 'what is the purpose of its creativity?' Does it entail ethical and social goals? Is it about collective creativity or only the story of heroines and heroes?

The resurgent city

Remember, and this is now hard to believe, that in the 1970s many thought that cities had little hope as they would become hollowed out as industries declined and moved production to Asia and elsewhere. New York, as one example, nearly went bankrupt in the 1970s.

A significant phenomenon emerged in the transition to knowledge intensity from the early 1980s onwards. The city began again to exert a gravitational pull, because of its resources in learning, its capacity to help exchange and transactions, its cultural institutions and richer artistic life and vibrancy, its stock of buildings and infrastructure and its transport links, and it is here that knowledge is clustered. The city was seen as an accelerator of opportunity. The city is a dense communications system that is not easy to replicate in other settings. Once the urban focus re-emerged, a vast urban regeneration process began with the tearing down of the past to make the city ready for professional-services-related industries, offices and residential developments that frequently pushed out older tenants as a result of the gentrification process. Often the results were negative. Simultaneously an extensive retrofitting exercise began.

Many cities concluded 'we need a new vision', a narrative or compelling story about where to go and how to get there. Discussions have been intense about the best way to create this picture of the future.

Urban visioning

What urban visions say and how they are put together has changed over time, as have the people whose creative input has been asked for. Taking a sweep through history and looking at the origins, we can see that planning has mostly been top-down. City making was originally more authoritarian and perhaps even dictatorial. This is how Paris was completely reshaped by Haussmann based on the edict of the king in 19th-century France. It then became systematized, bureaucratic and usually centralized, and in many places it still is. When city planning itself developed as a professional discipline it was largely closed, and planning was determined by 'experts' often specializing in areas like land use, road building or engineering. There was little communication with those affected by the plans. There has been a challenge to this approach over the last 30 years.

The newer city visioning increasingly began to focus on partnerships, initially between the public sector and business interests. More recently there has been a drive to make planning more participatory and open, and to involve those directly touched by planning decisions and draw on their inventiveness in all its forms. Co-creation is the new watchword. This is for several reasons. First, there is the democratic impulse. Second, and perhaps more important, it is recognized that involving people in decisions about a city makes plans more sustainable. Things are cared for more as people feel appreciated and so develop pride; projects are sustained and last longer because they reflect local knowledge and often bring about new solutions that those at the centre would not be able to see.

Co-creation has become a powerful concept for the creative city agenda and in harnessing the collective imagination. It is now affecting economic, social, cultural and democratic life. Yet it reminds us that often significant ideas are neglected until 'the time is right'. The co-creation timeline started in the late 1960s with the workplace democracy movement in Sweden giving workers the right to co-design IT systems that impacted on their work – then called cooperative co-design. Americans took up the idea in the 1970s, calling it participatory design as cooperative sounded too collectivist. Watchwords followed, such as collaborative enquiry, and by the 1980s collaborative place-making or planning, user-centred design and co-creative fact-finding were being discussed.

The work of professors C.K. Prahalad and Venkatram Ramaswamy was key by coining the term co-creation (Prahalad and Ramaswamy 2000). By 2000 studies on co-creation found that those involved in co-creative processes experienced greater individual competence, support for out-comes, better legitimacy of the process and strengthened social net-works. Allied to this is the development of the 'open innovation' idea. In 2006 Jeff Howe coined the word 'crowdsourcing', so reinforcing the breakdown of barriers and the notion that it is not only the expert who has knowledge (Howe 2006).

The essence of crowdsourcing is an old idea in new clothing, remind-ing us that the creative spark can be bringing back something old. Think here, from many examples, of the longitude problem, which made sailing difficult and dangerous, and the Longitude Prize. In 1714 the British government offered the then significant sum of £20,000 for a solution. Considered perhaps unsolvable, John Harrison, the son of a carpenter, won the prize by inventing the marine chronometer, an accurate, vacuum-sealed pocket watch.

Increasingly the creation of city visions in Europe, North America and Australasia began to involve wider consultation and partnership working. This is in part because past planning was seen to have failed and to have created urban environments that are unsatisfactory and soulless. Cars still dominate and have encouraged an urban sprawl with little identity. Public opinion is now so strong that decision makers have no choice but to do more than inform, and to instead consult and ideally co-create. Consulting widely can be time consum-ing and can raise expectations of what is possible, causing intense discussions. The consensus, however, is that more is to be gained from consulting than lost.

An age-old dilemma remains. Do you get a stronger, more imaginative vision from one person or a small leadership group or from wider con-sultation or a mixed partnership of public, civic and private interests?

Is vision from above better than that from below? Clearly China or countries in the Middle East have been able to undertake projects of dramatic grandeur and scale. Whether these are liveable places is a different question. In essence, these are driven from above. The type of city making recently witnessed there is unlikely to emerge from a local visioning exercise. The historical development of regeneration agencies reveals these dilemmas and reminds us whose imagination is involved in city development and of what kind.

Version one of post-war urban renewal was wholesale razing to the ground and the displacement of local communities. The first recognized programme in Pittsburgh in 1950 demolished a large section of the downtown heart and created the Golden Triangle, a process which James Baldwin, the novelist, dubbed 'negro removal'. Renewal plans mostly involved driving expressways through city centres to ease routes to the suburbs. In 1961 Jane Jacobs published *The Death and Life of Great American Cities*, one of the first critiques of contemporary large-scale urban renewal. Jacobs understood the subtle cultural ecology of neighbourhoods and cities. Her work began to gain traction by the 1970s, when organized movements began to resist tearing communities apart through highway construction.

Arthur Ziegler, co-founder of the Pittsburgh History and Landmarks Foundation in 1964, started fighting his city hall and big developers. He was inspired by Jacobs, who said Pittsburgh was being 'witlessly murdered'. Pittsburgh's city centre today is no longer being planned chiefly for cars and sterile towers, but instead on the needs of pedestrians, cyclists and mass transit. Historic preservation is preferred over the demolition approach to urban development. Ziegler's foundation helped rebuild the varied streetscapes Jacobs championed. He notes: 'There's almost nobody walking in Gateway Center. They're all across the street with the old buildings, the shops and restaurants.'[2]

Urban renewal *version two*, predominantly present in the 1980s/1990s, was still largely physically driven, such as in London or Melbourne Docklands. Here it is the architect and urban designer who take the leading role in imagining what a place could become, rather than wider sources of creativity.

---

2 https://www.pittsburghmagazine.com/Pittsburgh-Magazine/August-2016/Deep-In-The-Heart-of-Downtown/.

It was clear that their Docklands needed rethinking for new purposes, as the nature of shipping through containerization had changed and the ports had become redundant and moved. Vast spaces were emptied out, providing new opportunities. The local authorities, perhaps lacking courage to move forward, had let these areas stagnate, and this was perceived as an absence of civic leadership.

The British and Victorian governments stepped in and, bypassing local democracy and their planning procedures, imposed external developmental agencies that acted in a far more focused way to deliver regeneration with the help of additional government resources. This was both a negative and a positive experience. Positive in that they just got on with it. In both cases there was criticism of the results as they were not able to meet the challenge of developing city-making strategies that involved top-down and bottom-up approaches simultaneously. Their visions were more about gleaming towers and business parks, with local communities mostly absent from decision making.

The London Docklands Development Corporation (LDDC) was set up in 1981 and disbanded in 1998, when its powers were handed to local authorities. One of its main achievements was Canary Wharf, which moved the financial district of London further eastwards along the Thames with this vision of gleaming towers. This catalyst undoubtedly helped to dramatically transform the East End of London, with Docklands Light Railway and London City Airport completely changing connectivity. That aside, the relatively dull, suburban redevelopments, pockmarked with out of town shopping centres beyond in places like Beckton, speak of missed opportunities in good placemaking, added to which poverty still sits side by side with great wealth creation and upmarket housing. Several commentators believe LDDC fell short by placing too much emphasis on the private sector[3] instead of working through the more complicated process of blending the older community into the emerging new Docklands.

In Melbourne,[4,5] contrary to the 'visions' to create more human-centred, socially inclusive, mixed communities, business interests

---

3 https://www.citymetric.com/fabric/after-thirty-years-canary-wharf-how-has-it-changed-geogra phy-east-london-3565. See also Foster (1999).

4 https://www.development.vic.gov.au/projects/docklands.

5 https://www.theage.com.au/national/victoria/can-docklands-be-put-back-together-again-2012 0302-1u82a.html.

determined the outcomes too strongly, as they exerted substantial control and built a windswept, vertical city with minimal life at street level. The occasional element of public art – artwash – is not really able to redeem such a narrow vision. It could have been a model of sustainable development, with the community helping to shape the area. The City of Melbourne, the local government authority for central Melbourne that represents a broader public interest, was frozen out of decision making for over a decade, and once back with authority immediately created a 'Community and Place Plan'.[6]

Urban visioning *version three* has developed over the last two decades, and a different vocabulary has emerged, such as we want 'sustainable development', 'a high quality of life', 'a well-educated population', 'good roads and public transport' and 'to attract and retain talent'. Perhaps 20 years ago this might have sounded forward-looking, but who today would want 'unsustainable development' or 'a less educated workforce'? These are now the globally accepted standards embedded in agreements such as Habitat III of 2016 and the UN's 2030 Agenda and its 17 Sustainable Development Goals (SDGs),[7] where goal 11 focuses on cities, highlighting the need for them to be 'inclusive, safe, resilient and sustainable'. The creative challenge today is to embed these SDGs into the basic way that cities maintain themselves and develop.

The additional visionary element is the 'extra', or the thing which your city is doing that is different or special. What that is will depend on the aspirations and desires of each city. In terms of being more sustainable, that might mean to be much greener than the SDGs suggest; likewise, to be really inclusive would involve shared decision making. For instance, it is often illegal for citizens to improve or maintain public spaces, parks, abandoned buildings and other urban commons that impact upon their lives. In 2014 Bologna adopted the 'Regulation on Collaboration between Citizens and the City for the Care and Regeneration of Urban Commons' and launched 'the city as a commons' project. This is a significant creative innovation providing a legal and administrative framework for citizens to directly care for their urban commons.[8] This is more radical than the quadruple helix approach to city making that involves four partners (the public sector,

---

6 https://www.melbourne.vic.gov.au/community/strong-communities/Pages/docklands-community-and-place-plan.aspx.

7 https://sustainabledevelopment.un.org/?menu=1300.

8 https://www.theguardian.com/cities/2015/jun/15/urban-common-radical-community-gardens.

private sector, universities and people), as the latter is essentially voluntary whereas Bologna's declaration is enshrined in regulation.

This regulation embodies the notion of 'the right to and responsibility for the city' and the participative imperatives and agendas related to it. City making at its best is a joint endeavour where citizens feel they are real shapers and makers.

The central difference between a more creative approach and a traditional one to visioning is that in the latter people usually say 'we will review things, but these are the rules', and so the vision is constrained and determined by existing rules. In the former the vision is created in a more unconstrained way and the question then asked is 'what rules need rethinking and readjusting to achieve our vision?'

Visioning is essentially about storytelling – to oneself as well as to others. It is a powerful tool that puts the whole brain to work stimulating a desire to connect threads and narrate a causal sequence of events. It can drive motivation if those who hear it have a sense that they have a role and can be a participant in how it unfolds – be they a public servant, a civic activist or a businessperson. To create urban visions that can gain traction across population groups, divides and interests is complex. It involves the art of mediation, the ability to deal with conflict, and creative processes are often the best way to bring out the unheard voices, to draw out the deeper visceral feelings that drive the way people understand the world.

The rise of wicked problems

This unfolding world, driven largely by the logic of capitalism, has created a raft of intractable problems. These include an economic model that threatens the ability to operate within planetary boundaries, the need to decarbonize the economy, the lack of will to address ever-growing urban populations, the need to adopt a 'cradle to cradle' approach to business so that waste becomes a resource for something else, rethinking food systems and how food is produced to reduce obesity, endemic deprivation and poverty in some cities. In addition, the urban dynamic has made some cities impoverished with under-educated populations, and few attraction poles or resources, skills and opportunities (Collier 2008). If treated seriously the problems need to reshape our patterns of thinking, planning, behaviour and managing

– this in itself would be a creative act and reminds us of the new urgency for imagination, inventiveness and creativity and for the courage needed to act.

This is the landscape of new complex wicked problems – issues that cut across many public policy problems. Wicked problems are seemingly intractable, made up of interrelated dilemmas and issues that interweave political, economic and social questions. They cannot be tackled by traditional approaches where problems are simply defined, analysed and solved in sequential steps. They have characteristics that make traditional, hierarchical, top-down thinking less adept at solving them. There is no definite or unique 'correct' way of viewing or formulating the problem, and different stakeholders see the problem and solutions differently, often having deeply held ideological views. Data is frequently uncertain, difficult to acquire or missing. Wicked problems are connected to other problems, and every solution reveals new aspects of the problem that needs adjusting. The greatest impact of creativity comes when it finds a way of solving wicked problems.

The creative city notion remains both contentious and compelling. Some think we talk too much about creativity, others say its value is only beginning to be recognized, and yet others talk of the creativity crisis.[9,10] Some worry that 'creativity' is too fashionable (Mould 2018), thoughtlessly applied without detailed understanding of its potential and what its broader scope could be. Consequently, people get bored and think about the 'next big thing'. In terms of cities, this means concepts such as 'the learning city', 'the liveable city', 'the smart city' or 'the innovative city'.

A cautionary note is crucial, and it relates to the problem of hype. The severe danger in constantly emphasizing creativity or innovations is that we develop the latter for their own sake without any real purpose. They may have little utility or fail to deal with important needs. The aim is simply to pump up desires by dreaming up ever-changing fashions and trends. You could call this misplaced creativity. There is

---

9 An IBM 2010 Global CEO Study concludes that creativity is the most important leadership quality for success, with 60 per cent of the 1500 private and public sector leaders participating in the one-on-one interviews saying this.

10 Ted Schwarzrock's study traced 300 000 US children for 50 years and concluded that since 1990 creativity has been declining – see https://ibmcai.com/2015/04/16/our-creativity-crisis/.

much of this. We should, of course, generate new solutions to many challenges, yet at times the creative response may well be to hold back and to ask ourselves 'do we need this particular innovation?'

Simultaneously there is a paradox: the more we discuss creativity, the more we focus on a culture of risk aversion. The evaluation of everything from a perspective of risk is a defining characteristic of contemporary society. Risk is the managerial paradigm and default mechanism that has embedded itself into how companies, community organizations and the public sector operate. Risk is a prism through which any activity is judged. Risk has its experts, consultants, interest groups, specialist literature, an associational structure and lobbying bodies. A risk industry has formalized itself. It is similar to how acute awareness of marketing emerged as a core idea to operate business over 50 years ago.

Risk subtly encourages us to constrain aspirations, act with over-caution, avoid challenges and be sceptical about thinking afresh. It narrows our world into a defensive shell. The life of a community self-consciously concerned with risk and safety is different from one focused on discovery, exploration and inventive problem solving.

Risk consciousness is a growth industry; hardly a day passes without some new risk being noted. It is as if risk hovers over individuals like an independent force waiting to strike the unsuspecting citizen. The notion of an accident seems to have gone from our vocabulary. Cleansing the world of accidents means scouring the world for someone to blame. This is the landscape of risk.

There is the frenzy problem. Everyone is responding to a world that has changed dramatically. It feels like a paradigm shift, and people want to be able to cope, companies want to know what to do and cities want answers and solutions to their complex problems. While many things seem the same, everyone knows their underlying operating dynamics are different. There is a proliferating global craze as places want to evolve to, or simply claim that they are, a 'creative city' or a 'smart city'. These seem like answers to coping with this transition. But often people want creativity or smart solutions to solve more problems than they can cope with. Importantly many problems or opportunities do not necessarily require creativity per se. The central point is to have a mindset willing to reassess things openly and to be creative when necessary.

In sum, *there is a systemic challenge focusing on five interconnected dilemmas,* all of which cluster in cities:

- The *risk nexus* and its consequences, including having the governance capacity and the determination and courage to deal with it even though this will upset some entrenched interests. This involves the maintenance of energy, water and food security and the sustainable and circular management of natural resources for a growing and increasingly urban population, and doing so with a population that is increasingly diverse, where issues of cultural identity rise sharply to the fore, all with stretched public resources.
- The inability of the *current economic order* to provide the equality and stability citizens increasingly demand and to satisfy their yearning and desire to bend the market dynamic towards bigger public purposes. Many believe that market-based decision making on its own is an impoverished theory of choice making. It creates an economy that is 'materially expansive, socially divisive and environmentally hostile'. To avoid crisis turning into collapse, a fundamental rethink of the structure and operation of the current economic system is necessary. This will affect lifestyles and societies, and there will be resistance.
- *Another pattern of growth* is required that ensures we operate within planetary boundaries as well as provide the ability to create wealth and innovations. This is the promise of the 'fourth industrial revolution for the earth' and other evolving models such as 'doughnut economics'.
- The ability to *guide the digitizing age* and the evolving fourth industrial revolution in a human-centred way as technologies fuse and blur the lines between the physical, the digital and the biological spheres, and where the digital is embedded within societies and even the human body. Guiding that age should focus too on the ability to use digital possibilities to refresh democratic processes and help citizens become city makers.
- Addressing our sense of identity as to *where we belong* when everything is on the move in our more nomadic world where there is more mixing and migration flows are growing. Populism is one expression as the world turns to its darker face and tensions between our social and our tribal selves grow.

Given these important issues, some rightly criticize the creative city or smart city notions, claiming on one hand that there is too much focus on narrow groups like artists or those in the media, design and performance industries, and on the other that it is the techno-nerds driving development. In both cases the essential question is 'what are the specific qualities of artistic creativity, or the creative economy, or technology apps, that might help establish a better city?'

Others say these notions simply help to spectacularize the city to attract the 'creative class', that raft of knowledge workers and researchers who are crucial to developing a more knowledge-intensive, driven economy. They say this reinforces divisions between rich and poor, taking away the focus from the less privileged rather than looking at their entrenched problems in an imaginative way. While this segment of the population is crucial, representing perhaps 25 to 30 per cent of the people in a country's centrally located cities, they do not represent the totality of a city's creative forces. The over-strong emphasis on this group is unfortunate.

Urban creativity is more than this. The better question is 'what can the other 75 per cent of apparently "non-creative" people contribute to a better city?' To be an urban success:

> Cities have one crucial resource – their people. Human cleverness, desires, motivations, imagination and creativity are replacing location, natural resources and market access as urban resources. The creativity of those who live in and run cities will determine future success. Of course, this has always been critical to cities' ability to survive and adapt. Cities when they became large and complex enough to present problems of urban management became laboratories to develop the solutions – technological, conceptual and social – to their problems of growth and change. (Landry 2000)

The key priorities for our curiosity, imagination, creativity, knowledge or innovations or smart apps today are how to create the fourth, clean, green, lean industrial revolution, to encourage intercultural understanding, to help reduce the rich–poor divide and to create ambition and meaning beyond consumerism.

References

Bell, Daniel (1973), *The Coming of Post-Industrial Society: A Venture in Social Forecasting*, New York: Basic Books.

Collier, Paul (2008), *The Future of Capitalism: Facing the New Anxieties*, New York: Harper.

Drucker, Peter (1969), *The Age of Discontinuity*, London: Butterworth-Heinemann.

Foster, Janet (1999), *Docklands: Cultures in Conflict, Worlds in Collision*, London: UCL Press.

Howe, Jeff (2006), 'The rise of crowdsourcing', *Wired Magazine*, **14** (6), June.

Landry, Charles (2000), *The Creative City: A Toolkit for Urban Innovators*, London: Earthscan.

Machlup, Fritz (1962), *The Production and Distribution of Knowledge in the United States*, Princeton, NJ: Princeton University Press.

Mould, Olli (2018), *Against Creativity*, London: Verso.

Prahalad, C.K. and Venkat Ramaswamy (2000), 'Co-opting customer competence', *Harvard Business Review*, January/February.

Touraine, Alain (1971), *The Post-Industrial Society. Tomorrow's Social History: Classes, Conflicts and Culture in the Programmed Society*, New York: Random House.

5 Objective and subjective: my story

This text is written from the perspective of someone heavily involved in the creativity movement and a practitioner. It is as objective as I can make it since I have been perhaps the main instigator of the creative city development idea since its origins in the late 1980s. The advantage is that 'I was there' and an active participant, both practically seeking to help cities unleash their potential, but also writing about it. This involved persuading people and cities that the topic had relevance; discussing inventive solutions to dilemmas that revitalizing depressed urban areas can create, such as gentrification; working with many thoughtful collaborators and at the same time reflecting on that work and that of critics. This resulted in innumerable reports and several books over a 30-year period, and this publication draws on that work. The link below to my archive goes into the hundreds of projects I have undertaken, many with my colleagues at Comedia, an organization I set up in 1978.[1,2]

The disadvantage is that some might feel this is a subjective account and that I might not be self-critical enough. This could be true, especially since I take issue with some of the ways the creative cities agenda has developed over the world that shifted from my original intent. Throughout the history of the creative city notion there has been a tension between a broader aim to change the overall dynamics of places and a narrower aim whereby the arts and creative economy sectors stand as a proxy for all creativity. The former aim would be to develop a 'culture of creativity' whereby people and organizations can feel empowered and where there is a 'yes, if' rather than a 'no, because' attitude. Yet you cannot control how an idea is read and interpreted nor how others take it and use it for their purposes. This is true of the 'creative city' notion.

---

1 http://charleslandry.com/.

2 http://charleslandry.com/resources-downloads/archive-of-talks-and-projects/.

A dozen years after the first explorations – around the year 2000 – the notion spread like a rash, with many places claiming to be creative when probably they were not. The words 'creative' and 'creative city' were overused and narrowly defined, with a danger that the concept would hollow out. In the meantime, other monikers or labels like 'knowledge' or 'smart' were witnessing the same fate. In addition, the exaggerated focus on the creative economy sectors or artists as the main source of creativity was harmful, important and inspirational as they can be. My life experience tells me that there are many other types of people who are imaginative and uplifting. What irritates me too is the way people identify themselves as 'I am a creative' when I think it is better for others to say you might be creative.

Personally, for me the core intent of the creative city idea as an urban strategy tool remains significant, and as I wrote in the first short book on the topic with Franco Bianchini in 1995, with whom I initially developed the overall ideas:

> We explain what is new about the interlocking crises facing many cities . . . and how new sets of problems have risen up the agenda, partly as a result of the decay of the old shared rhythms of life and work . . . and we ask what creativity is and how it can be harnessed to make city life better. We argue that the hard sciences of urban planning need to be enriched by mobilising the experiences of different disciplines and people currently marginalised from decision making. We explore what it means to be a creative city and set out both why creativity has become more important to cities and why nurturing it is important for economic success – and how creativity can be mobilised to help solve the myriad problems of the city, with lateral, synthetic, cross-disciplinary approaches, such as the importance of creative responses to urban problems, be they in traffic management, business development, greening the city, integrating ethnic communities, regenerating run-down housing estates or enlivening city centres. (Landry and Bianchini 1995)

As I said in the first acknowledgement pages of *The Creative City: A Toolkit for Urban Innovators* in 2000:

> It is a clarion call for us to think imaginatively to create opportunities and to solve problems. . . . It seeks to inspire people to think, plan and act creatively in the city and to get an ideas factory going. . . . Its aim is to make readers feel 'I can do that too', and to spread confidence that creative and innovative solutions to urban problems are feasible however bad they may seem at

first sight. A central message is that cities are changing dramatically in ways that amount to a paradigm shift. If we keep trying to solve urban problems with the old intellectual apparatus and mindset we will come up against the same obstacles. . . . Taking an eagle-eye view of cities around the world it is astonishing how many ordinary people show leadership qualities to make the extraordinary possible when given the chance. (Landry 2000)

The Chinese edition that followed shortly afterwards said:

The idea is aspirational; a clarion call to encourage open-mindedness and imagination. The intention is to have a dramatic impact on organizational culture. The philosophy of the 'creative city' is that there is always more potential in any place than any of us would think at first sight. It posits that conditions need to be created to imaginatively harness opportunities or address seemingly intractable urban problems. These might range from addressing homelessness, to creating wealth through developing a new business model, enhancing and beautifying the visual environment, reusing an old building to generating events to foster social bonding. It is a positive concept. (Landry 2003)

In the late 1980s and early 1990s I spent much time with Franco Bianchini, Colin Mercer and Bob McNulty, and later others, both in Europe and Australia, exploring issues of cities, culture, distinctiveness and creativity. One under-acknowledged person was David Yencken, who co-organized the first creative cities event in 1988 in Melbourne largely focused on the arts, but whose own view was much broader (Yencken 1988). The work of Peter Hall, the planning historian, along with his long-term interest in innovation and creativity and his personal encouragement, was crucial right from the beginning.

All these people became important contributors and critics of the evolving creative cities movement. It was an uphill struggle persuading local authorities, who were initially our main contact point, that issues of culture and creativity were important. It was when the link to economic development was made in the mid-1990s that a breakthrough happened.

Over the years there have been many supporters, helpful critics and detractors of the idea. There is a vast academic literature on the topic, which a quick Google Scholar search reveals.[3] I have found, for instance,

---

3 There are around 7000 citations of my various writings and similar numbers for other texts.

the finely textured critical academic work of Allen Scott (2000), Masayuki Sasaki (2001), Andy Pratt (2007), Justin O'Connor (2010), Michael Storper (1997), Barton Kunstler (2003), Paul Chatterton (2000), David Throsby (1994, 2000) and Jon Hawkes (2001) rewarding. Hawkes' short book *The Fourth Pillar of Sustainability: Culture's Essential Role in Public Planning* (2001) was very valuable.

The success of Richard Florida's book *The Rise of the Creative Class* in 2002 with its focus on the three Ts – talent, technology, tolerance – gave the creative city notion a boost, but pushed it into a different direction (Florida 2002). Again he had supporters and detractors, and many critics like Jamie Peck (2005) and Stephen Pritchard.[4] Florida was criticized for focusing on a specific 'creative class' and helping the gentrification of poorer areas by encouraging the hipster community to move into urban areas and pushing the original communities out. Another important book was John Howkins' *The Creative Economy: How People Make Money from Ideas* (2001). Critics conflate the three of us even though my work is specifically not about a 'creative class', and not only about the 'creative economy', but instead more about the creative ecosystem of a city and how it can empower people's potential. One thrust of the critique is that a neo-liberal agenda is being pursued. I do not recognize myself here, but perhaps I suffer from 'false consciousness'. You as a reader can be the judge.

References

Chatterton, Paul (2000), 'Will the real creative city please stand up?', *City*, **4** (3), 390–97.
Florida, Richard (2002), *The Rise of the Creative Class: And How It's Transforming Work, Leisure, Community and Everyday Life*, New York: Basic Books.
Hawkes, Jon (2001), *The Fourth Pillar of Sustainability: Culture's Essential Role in Public Planning*, Melbourne: Common Ground, in association with the Cultural Development Network.
Howkins, John (2001), *The Creative Economy: How People Make Money from Ideas*, London: Penguin Books.
Kunstler, Barton (2003), *The Hothouse Effect: Intensify Creativity in Your Organization Using Secrets from History's Most Innovative Communities*, New York: AMACOM/ American Management Association.
Landry, Charles (2000), *The Creative City: A Toolkit for Urban Innovators*, London: Earthscan.

---

4 See Stephen Pritchard (2018), who likes to refer to me as 'a peddlar of gentrification': http:// colouringinculture.org/blog/placeguarding.

Landry, Charles (2003), *The Creative City: A Toolkit for Urban Innovators*, Beijing: Tsinghua University Press.

Landry, Charles and Franco Bianchini (1995), *The Creative City*, London: Demos (in association with Comedia). Available at https://www.demos.co.uk/files/thecreativecity.pdf.

O'Connor, Justin (2010) *The Cultural and Creative Industries: A Literature Review*, 2nd edn, Creativity, Culture and Education Series, Newcastle: Creativity, Culture and Education.

Peck, J. (2005), 'Struggling with the creative class', *International Journal of Urban and Regional Research*, **29** (4), 740–70.

Pratt, Andy (2007), 'The state of the cultural economy: The rise of the cultural economy and the challenges to cultural policy making', in António Pinot Ribeiro (ed.), *The Urgency of Theory*, Manchester: Carcanet Press/Gulbenkin Foundation, pp. 166–90.

Pritchard, Stephen (2018), 'Place guarding: Activist art against gentrification', in Cara Courage and Anita McKeown (eds), *Creative Placemaking: Research, Theory and Practice*, London: Routledge, pp. 140–55.

Sasaki, Masayuki (2001), *The Challenge for the Creative City*, Tokyo: Iwanami Shoten.

Scott, Allen J. (2000), *The Cultural Economy of Cities: Essays on the Geography of Image-Producing Industries*, Los Angeles, CA: University of California.

Storper, Michael (1997), *The Regional World: Territorial Development in a Global Economy*, New York: The Guilford Press.

Throsby, David (1994), 'The production and consumption of the arts: A view of cultural economics', *Journal of Economic Literature*, XXXII, 1–29.

Throsby, David (2000), *Economics and Culture*, Cambridge: Cambridge University Press.

Yencken, David (1988), 'The creative city', *Meanjin*, **47** (4).

6 A timeline and trajectory

The more recent historical timeline helps us understand how the concepts and ideas of the creative city idea evolved and progressed. Without this it is difficult to grasp how the various elements described in the sections below fit together and why people have differing ideas about what a creative city is. Franco Bianchini's lengthy article 'Reflections on the origins, interpretations and development of the creative city idea' (2018) summarizes this helpfully from his perspective in great detail.

In the early 1980s people began to look at the link between specific geographic locations, their cultures and their creativity in defining a place. The creative city concept built on a number of trajectories including Gunnar Törnqvist's (1983) notion of the 'creative milieu' – a term first used by Hippolyte Taine in 1865 (Hall 1998) – and Phillippe Aydalot and colleagues investigating innovative milieux at GREMI (Aydalot 1986). Åke Andersson, a regional economist, in 1985 published an important account of creativity and city development using Stockholm as a case study, as well as looking at creativity and economic development in a regional context (1987).

Less known in the English-speaking world, their work had a different trajectory and did not consider issues like old buildings, cultural activities or the emerging cultural or creative industries. They discussed instead the context of knowledge and regional development and drew attention to the role of the creative environment. When Törnqvist developed the notion of the 'creative milieu' he noted four key features: information transmitted among people; knowledge (based partly on the storage of information); competence in certain relevant activities; and creativity (the creation of something new as an outcome of the former three activities).

Peter Hall, from the 1960s onwards, looked at regional development and summarized his long-term work in his magisterial book *Cities in*

Civilization (1998). Here he mapped 'great cities in their golden ages', such as Athens, Florence, London, Vienna, Paris and Berlin, before looking at 'the city as an innovative milieu', focusing on Manchester, Glasgow, Berlin, London, Detroit, San Francisco/Palo Alto and Tokyo-Kanagawa.

Apart from Peter Hall, most looked at high-tech clusters – often dubbed technology or science parks – that felt clean and sanitized and were mostly located at the edge of cities. Silicon Valley was the pioneer in the late 1950s, as was Akademgorodok near Novosibirsk in Russia, then Sophia Antipolis near Nice in the 1960s, Tsukuba in Japan in the 1970s and many Chinese ones in the 1980s, as well as the several technopolises in the Nordic countries in the 1990s. Hall, by contrast, understood that the urban context with its dense networks was crucial to fostering innovation and exchange, as in places from New York to Tokyo and beyond.

Peter Hall's contribution was crucial in legitimizing the idea of the creative city. Given his status, credibility and track record, Hall gave 'energy and confidence' to the group working on the creative city idea from the later 1980s onwards. He approached me as early as 1989 to work together on a consultancy report titled *London: World City Moving into the 21st Century* (Kennedy 1991). I then went on to assess the cultural power and position of New York, Los Angeles, Paris, London and Tokyo on behalf of the research group. Later, in 1998, we together wrote *Innovative and Sustainable European Cities*, which trialled a number of models to assess the degree of innovativeness of a large number of projects in Europe (Hall and Landry 1998). This foreshadowed the shift to seeing creativity and innovation in other realms such as greening the economy or planning practice.

Jane Jacobs was an important early figure here in shifting the focus away from wholesale demolition of urban areas to be replaced by urban motorways or soulless towers (Jacobs 1961). She highlighted how the subtle complex ecology of place fostered interactions, economic vibrancy, civic life and belonging. This helped change the urban planning paradigm and prefigured many of the arguments made later about creative places. As Sharon Zukin notes: 'She was the person who, against all odds in the mid-twentieth century, extolled the messiness, the grittiness, the tentativeness, but also the firm friendships of city life.'[1]

---

1 https://www.citsee.eu/interview/naked-city-authenticity-and-urban-citizenship-interview-sharon-zukin.

In 1988 two important international conferences were held which linked the arts and the cultural industries to the city. The first, organized by the British American Arts Association in Glasgow, was called 'Arts and the changing city: An agenda for urban regeneration'. The second, in Melbourne, was called 'Creative city', and focused on how arts and cultural concerns could be better integrated into the planning process for city development. While largely focused on the arts, it included a speech by David Yencken (1988) where he argues cities must be efficient and fair, but also committed to fostering creativity among its citizens and to providing emotionally satisfying places and experiences for them.

During exactly the same period, without knowledge of each other at that time, my colleague Franco Bianchini and I at Comedia began establishing the creative city notion as a practical urban policy tool that saw creativity as a resource for urban development. This included the imagination of artists, scientists, businesses and ordinary people, as well as the civic creativity of public officials defined as imaginative problem solving applied to public good objectives.

An important moment in the creative city trajectory from the early 1980s onwards was when the arts community started to justify their economic worth and calculate its impact on the economy. The trigger for doing this was the economic crisis of the late 1970s and early 1980s that had the effect of reducing their funding and income. There was pressure to justify public investment in the arts. This began in the United States and later expanded to the United Kingdom and Australia, and in the 1990s it spread to Europe and elsewhere.

Early actors involved were Partners for Livable Places in Washington, where the founder Robert McNulty was encouraged by Harvey Perloff in 1979 to launch a programme to document the economic value of design and cultural amenities, calculating initially in Los Angeles the value of cultural activities excluding the film industry. Their 'Economics of Amenity'[2] programme beginning in the early 1980s illustrated how cultural activities and amenities and the quality of life in a community are linked to economic development and job creation. This led Partners to promote the idea of 'cultural planning'. Another early study, the first of its kind, was undertaken by Patricia Jones in 1982 on behalf of the Port Authority in New York, the study being called *The Arts as an*

---

2 http://livable.org/livability-resources/22/275-economics-of-amenity.

Industry: Their Importance to the New York–New Jersey Metropolitan Region.[3] In Britain, John Myerscough's *The Economic Importance of the Arts in Britain* (1988) made a mark, as did his follow-up study on Glasgow (Myerscough et al. 1988).

Already from the late 1970s onwards, the United Nations Educational, Scientific and Cultural Organization (UNESCO) and the Council of Europe had begun to investigate the cultural industries in general. They looked at not only the largely grant-aided arts sector, but in particular their commercial manifestations and their contribution to the economy. From the perspective of cities, Nick Garnham, an academic, was important. He was seconded to the Greater London Council in 1983/4 and set up a specialist cultural industries unit which put the cultural industries on the urban policy agenda. He argued that the alternative media and arts scene should focus on commercial viability; the market and real audiences had positive benefits and potentially would have far greater impact on changing the media landscape than remaining oppositional. This thinking and specialist unit idea was copied by many other cities. As a consequence, my organization, Comedia, produced many studies highlighting the power and potential of the sector in the changing world, in cities as diverse as London, Glasgow, Manchester, Birmingham and, later, other European cities, such as Barcelona, Cracow and beyond. A crucial shift had taken place. A key step was that the arts were increasingly seen as also part of industrial sectors, such as the music industry, which was predominantly commercial and did not look for public funding. Over time this led to the setting up of many economic development agencies with a focus on the cultural industries (later usually referred to as the creative industries).

Those studies showed that when you looked at music, the visual and performing arts, publishing or film together they represented an important employment and income sector. Later studies added museums and ancillary industries such as architectural services and auction houses to the calculations. These revealed that when you added together the whole supply chain the sector accounted for nearly 5 per cent of the economy in larger cities like Birmingham or Manchester, and more than 10 per cent for London or New York and Los Angeles. This array of economic impact studies was influential, and a significant moment

---

3 https://www.americansforthearts.org/by-program/reports-and-data/legislation-policy/naappd/the-arts-as-an-industry-their-economic-importance-to-the-new-york-new-jersey-metropolitan-region-0.

that got national policy makers engaged was when it was pointed out that in the early 1980s the exports of the music industry in Britain were larger than those of car manufacturing.

The effect of this kind of work became more pronounced over time as further impacts were drawn out – the spill over effects, such as the effect of the arts and culture on the image and identity of a place or on attracting tourists, and even later other soft factors such as the social impact of involvement in the arts on people's sense of empowerment, their confidence and their competence. The notion that the creativity of these wide groups was important for the city and the economy slowly became accepted. This increasing mountain of evidence gave comfort to economic development entities and sceptics.

In parallel, the changing nature of the global economy, and overall restructuring with its resulting changing terms of trade as production moved to Asia and especially China, focused minds. This shift was enabled by significant advances in new communications technologies and reduced transportation costs. As a consequence, cities in the West, especially Europe and North America, needed to move from being more reliant on industrial production to more reliant on creating knowledge-rich products and services based on research and the availability of highly skilled people. They needed to add value to every activity.

This dynamic process left many decision makers confused as they searched for new answers while their cities were physically locked into their past. The structure of their cities determined where housing was based and the type of housing to fulfil industrial needs, or the nature of transportation to ensure the logistics of production worked well, and everywhere there were old industrial structures.

There were vast industrial structures in search of new uses and roles, often surrounded by immense, underutilized, degraded areas. These had to be rethought to be fit for purpose for 21st-century needs. In this process areas were being replanned with the needs of the new evolving economy in mind.

Once the shift took hold all over the world, there were empty industrial buildings and factories. A massive movement of urban renewal and redevelopment began. Some wanted to raze everything to the ground and to start afresh. Others thought this was simplistic, because in the process you erase memory. This sense of loss, they argued, would be cruel and have negative downstream effects. They proposed instead to selectively reuse the old fabric.

The movement to revalue industrial heritage was triggered by conservationists, and the cultural community helped. Worldwide, several hundred old warehouses; breweries; train, bus or fire stations; cement, coal, textile, tobacco or steel factories; old markets; or military barracks were transformed into culture or experience centres, incubators and company breeding grounds, co-working spaces and hubs for wider urban regeneration.

Typically they were reused as incubators for the new sectors or as artist studios. In part this was because they were cheap, as they were next to the urban centre or in more peripheral areas in need of renewal as the old industries had died. Designers, musicians or artists were the pioneers or urban explorers who found the grungy, messy and unfinished feeling of these areas attractive and inspiring, especially since they had large, flexible spaces. They felt they could help make and shape these changing environments. Since no new uses had up to then been found, the authorities were keen to let this happen, often providing very good financial terms.

Perhaps most importantly the old buildings resonated with history, embodied a culture of the place and its work, and exuded memory, and their good build quality meant they had a strong personality. You could see the patina of the ages etched into their physical fabric. Often these large structures also included performance spaces or gallery venues. Overall they created an informal environment that attracted cafés and restaurants. In essence the pioneers made these areas popular and safer, and so they began to entice more conventional businesses to relocate, from software engineers to professional services like lawyers. Over time adjacent buildings would typically be revived and new structures built. The creative people who started the process in effect helped increase property prices, which meant traditional developers were willing to build, so increasing overall prices. The danger of this gentrification process was that those who initially made it happen were often pushed out as prices rose.

It is strange that those same places that had horrible working conditions are celebrated as places for the new and the hip. Why do these structures resonate? They exude memory and the patina of ages in an age where novelty increasingly erases memory. Typically their spaces are large and allow for flexibility and interesting structures.

Early examples of this type of development included the Zeche Zollverein in Essen or Duisburg Landschafts Park, both in the Ruhr; the Custard Factory in Birmingham; the Ufa Studios in Berlin; the Cable Factory, Nokia's former headquarters in Helsinki; or areas such as Temple Bar in Dublin and Merchant City in Glasgow. In Western Europe at the time, and in North America and Australasia, this kind of development became part of the urban development repertoire, repeated hundreds of times.

More recent examples include the Distillery District and Liberty Village in Toronto, the Museums Quartier in Vienna, Halles De Schaerbeek in Brussels, Granville Island in Vancouver, the refurbishment of old industrial buildings in Pyrmont Ultimo in Sydney and the Truman Brewery area around Brick Lane in London. In addition, after Eastern Europe transformed and opened up in 1989, more examples have emerged, like Pekarna in Maribor or Metelkovo Ljubljana, both in Slovenia. Trans Europe Halles is an association of such projects and 798 in Beijing is a Chinese example of a vast old factory complex turned into a hip arts place, with many galleries and the like.

The first urban project with 'creative city' in its title was 'Making the most of Glasgow's cultural assets: The creative city and its cultural economy', commissioned by the Scottish Development Agency in 1991.[4] This focused on the city as a creative organism and how it might use its historic assets as well as the city as a setting for developing creative industry sectors like design or music. However, a series of projects in Birmingham in 1988 prefigured the wider theme, including 'Establishing a media zone and a media enterprise centre in Birmingham' in 1988. This equally focused on how underused industrial buildings could be repurposed, and one result was the setting up of the Custard Factory.

In work with Glasgow, Comedia proposed a method of assessing the strengths and weaknesses of the cultural and creative sectors. It started with 'beginnings'. This is the stage which is concerned with 'ideas generation'. It is the initial moment and forum of 'creativity', whether this be during informal discussions of ideas in the home, street or

---

4 http://charleslandry.com/resources-downloads/archive-of-talks-and-projects/.

classroom or in the more formal processes of establishing patents or copyright. The 'production' phase then asks how is 'creativity' turned into products? Are the people, resources, productive capacities and training available to aid the transformation of ideas into marketable products? These people include impresarios, artistic directors, managers, producers, performers, designers, editors and engineers, as well as suppliers and makers of equipment, such as film or photo labs or studios, frame makers and scenery makers. A training infrastructure is necessary to provide the appropriate skills base for each sector. The third stage, 'circulation', concerns the availability of agents and agencies, distributors and wholesalers (say in film or publishing), or middle persons, packagers and assemblers of product. It also includes what catalogues, directories, archives, stock inventories and media outlets exist to aid the sale and circulation of cultural product. It involves too the role of cultural producers. Fourth are the 'delivery mechanisms' which are 'platforms' to allow cultural product to be consumed and enjoyed: it is about the places they are seen, experienced, consumed or bought online or offline. It means assessing the availability of theatres, cinemas, bookshops, concert halls, channels and screens, magazines, museums, public and community spaces, record shops and so on. With the rise of the Internet this has dramatically changed, with far more materials, whether written documents or films, available online. Lastly, there are 'audiences and reception'. This concerns the public and critics and other 'gatekeepers', and involves activities such as marketing, advertising and publicity. It involves assessments of issues such as market and audience research, as well as questions of pricing and sociological targeting (for example, young and old, gender and education). How good, for example, is the city at getting people from different economic and social backgrounds to participate in cultural activities? Or how good is the city/region at reaching overseas markets?

Comedia was not the only group working, thinking and writing about the notion of creative cities. In the early 1990s, Ray Cunningham from the Anglo-German Foundation for the Study of Industrial Society put Comedia in touch with Klaus Kunzmann, from the Institute for Spatial Planning at the University of Dortmund. He then brought into the discussion STADTart, a Dortmund-based cultural policy consultancy run by Ralf Ebert and Friedrich Gnad. Kunzmann's team had been exploring creativity themes through his work in Germany, and especially how cities can become more systematically creative. Kunzmann and STADTart studied the shift from traditional to more technologically advanced manufacturing and services in areas such as the Ruhr, and 'the impact of cultural and environmental industries on urban restructuring'. They had a significant influence on the creative city project.

In 1994 we gathered five German and five British cities (Cologne, Dresden, Unna, Essen and Karlsruhe and Bristol, Glasgow, Huddersfield, Leicester and Milton Keynes) together and held a three-day extended meeting in Glasgow, organized by Comedia and Klaus Kunzmann, to explore urban creativity. This resulted in a joint publication in 1996: *The Creative City in Britain and Germany* (Landry et al. 1996).

In 1995, a short book called *The Creative City*, which I wrote with Franco Bianchini, came out (Landry and Bianchini 1995). This considered how psychological research on creativity in individuals and organizations could be applied in urban policy. It defined creative thinking in opposition to 'instrumental rationality' and highlighted the 'synthetic' and 'holistic' nature of creativity. It was written as a handbook for policy makers, and suggested how obstacles to creativity could be removed and a creative milieu built. It discussed, based on examples, factors like handling capacity, valuing the contributions of immigrants, the use of catalyst events and processes, developing creative spaces, and balancing cosmopolitanism and localism. Importantly, it argued how creative city strategies have relevance well beyond the field of cultural policy, such as in education, transport, ecology, housing or health.

Both these publications broadened the notion of the creative city away from its more exclusive artistic and creative economy focus. They discussed issues like the organizational dynamics to foster creativity, what a creative milieu is and how you can encourage it, and what the role of history and tradition in creativity might be. A milestone that brought many of these themes together was the publication of *The Art of Regeneration: Urban Renewal through Cultural Activity* launched at a conference in Nottingham in 1996 (Landry et al. 1996).

While many of the ideas on the creative city were being developed in Britain, the first country to focus on and adopt the creativity theme was Australia, when in 1994 the prime minister, Paul Keating, launched a 'Creative Nation' cultural policy signalling the continent's openness to the world and its pride in its multicultural fabric. Australia saw culture as a resource for identity and the economy. It was also the first country to incorporate cultural resources and cultural planning thinking into practice. The 1992 plan developed by the Australian Local Government Association (ALGA) includes cultural planning along with economic, infrastructural, environmental and social planning among its imperatives for local government in Australia (ALGA 1992). The ALGA also developed a mechanism – Integrated Local Area Planning (ILAP) – to help implement this, and Brian Howe, then deputy prime minister under the Keating government, was crucial in providing resources to give the ILAP process some impact. 'Cultural planning' also began to be taken seriously in planning frameworks and to enter the language of urban planners and designers, local government officers, community arts workers and community organizations. Colin Mercer,[5] at the time Director of the Institute for Cultural Policy Studies at Griffith University, Brisbane, was important in advocating this new approach, and co-wrote *The Cultural Planning Handbook* in 1995 (Grogan et al. 1995). Jon Hawkes' *Fourth Pillar* book (2001) was significant in arguing that for the achievement of a sustainable and healthy society you needed a whole-of-government cultural framework, operating in parallel with social, environmental and economic frameworks.

Later, in Britain, Ken Robinson's 1999 report to the National Advisory Committee on Creative and Cultural Education, titled *All Our Futures: Creativity, Culture and Education*, was significant.[6] Its more radical agenda to emphasize the need for more creative education was seen as contentious, and was not taken up. This report clearly reminded us that our education system is largely responsible for how creative we become. It had a strong impact, as have his subsequent publications like his 2001 book *Out of Our Minds: Learning to Be Creative* (Robinson 2001).

The larger publication *The Creative City: A Toolkit for Urban Innovators* came out in 2000 and hit a nerve (Landry 2000). Its one sentence summary is 'When the world is changing dramatically we need to rethink the role of cities and their resources and how urban planning works.' Looking at examples from around the world, it described the evolution of a new urban world based on different principles from those that applied in industrial cities. It contrasted the 'urban engineering paradigm' of city development focused on hardware with 'creative city making' which emphasizes how understanding the software of the city

---

5 Mercer, Colin (2006), 'Cultural planning for urban development and creative cities', http://www.kulturplan-oresund.dk/pdf/Shanghai_cultural_planning_paper.pdf.

6 http://sirkenrobinson.com/pdf/allourfutures.pdf.

should shape how we build it. This was elaborated in *The Art of City Making* in 2006 (Landry 2006).

This work reflected an evolving planning paradigm from which later a global movement emerged buttressed by a series of creative city conferences, as in Glasgow (1994) mentioned previously, Amsterdam (1996), Helsinki (1998) and Huddersfield (2000), that reinforced the concept (Bianchini 2018; Grodach 2017).

The Huddersfield Creative Town Initiative (CTI) (see Wood and Taylor 2004), funded by £7 million from the European Union (EU) funded Urban Pilot Project in Kirklees, was the first comprehensive and explicit attempt to apply and embed the creative city principles across a whole city. It was managed by Phil Wood, who later became a partner in Comedia. The CTI launch event called 'Creative City. Why Cities Must Innovate to Survive' was a significant moment as several hundred people from across Europe and beyond became acquainted with the notion – especially as everyone received a free copy of my book *The Creative City: A Toolkit for Urban Innovators*.

The CTI project attempted to implement the idea of the 'cycle of urban creativity' (Landry 2000), a circular process linking five different stages: enhancing ideas-generating capacity; turning ideas into practice; networking and circulating ideas and practices; creating platforms for delivery; and building markets and audiences. There was some continuity with the 1990s but also some significant shifts. It was policy focused and involved some global organizations as well as UK ones. Unsurprisingly there was much greater emphasis on the digital economy, such as Charles Leadbeater's contribution on the 'weightless economy' and that of Ken Robinson on creativity's role in learning and in developing citizenship.

The geographer Paul Chatterton had an insightful critique of the Huddersfield conference, and of my 2000 book. He noted that the 'toolkit' approach favoured could direct people 'to opportunistic rather than strategic thinking, which can overlook or marginalise more structural problems faced by urban areas such as their place in the uneven flow of capital around the globe, lack of democratic accountability and an unsustainable growth of ecological footprints'. He was worried it would become 'little more than a rhetorical device which can placate the hearts and minds of local councillors and politicians that they are actually doing something whilst not doing anything at all' or that the rhetoric could be used by local elites as instruments to sanitize the city, to overlook growing social inequality and to promote more corporate urban environments, which neglect everyday and mundane forms of creativity and do not engage low-income residents (quoted in Bianchini 2018).

The idea, nevertheless, then caught a zeitgeist and got real traction for broader audiences from 2000 onwards. Prior to that it was the arts and cultural departments who took an interest, perhaps thinking 'if we say creative, we must be talking about artists'. Once economic development departments saw the value of the arts as an economic sector with multiple spin-offs on perception, image and attracting tourists, the concept began to take off. This left many questions unanswered, such as 'what about the intrinsic value of the arts or arts that challenge the status quo?' At the same time many people could not find a role in this evolving economy. Their skill set did not fit, which led in many places, in Allen Scott's words, to 'surface glitter and its underlying squalor' (2008).

A vital project for Comedia was the social impact of the arts programme – a series of ten research studies whose final book, written by Francois Matarasso in 1997, was *Use or Ornament?* (Matarasso 1997). This tried to redress the increasing economic focus of thinking and activity. The irony here is that we at Comedia had ourselves been one of the main promoters of breaking the fixed lines between the amateur, semi-professional and professional and the non-commercial and grant funded and the commercial. We acknowledged that subsidized cultural activity was often able to stretch boundaries, be provocative and raise difficult questions, but equally were not willing to accept that all commercial culture had little value. Many of these initial questions had been explored in the Comedia publications series from 1978 to 1985.

We felt, however, that policy makers were focusing too exclusively on the economic arguments that they felt more easily persuaded treasury ministries, investors and developers. This clearly had negative effects and shifted the whole creative city idea onto an economic agenda and property-led urban renewal, and downgraded its focus on issues of empowerment, cultural purpose and identity. The recoupling of social and economic agendas remains until today one of the most important battlegrounds.

The groundwork laid by an increasing number of studies on the impact of culture worldwide had a wider national impact. Persuaded by the mountain of economic evidence from the previous decade, the British government in 1998 became the first country to develop a national policy for the cultural industries, renaming them confusingly 'the creative industries' (since every industry is potentially creative, not only the music, design or film industries). Perhaps it was trying to avoid the political connotations of the word 'cultural' as the original advocates of the cultural industries were often alternative social movements, whose concern with identity and empowerment was at times challenging to the status quo.

The then British government undertook a major mapping exercise of the value of the sector through its Department of Culture, Media and Sports (DCMS), and its list included those industries who have an *'origin in individual creativity, skill and talent and have a potential for wealth and job creation through the generation and exploitation of intellectual property'* (DCMS 2001; italics in original). They deemed these to be advertising, architecture, arts and antique markets, crafts, design, designer fashion, film, video and photography, software, computer games and electronic publishing, music and the visual and performing arts, publishing, television and radio (DCMS 2001). The DCMS list has been influential, and many other nations have since formally adopted it. It has also been criticized, however; for instance, by dividing the field into sectors it underplays the differences between lifestyle businesses, non-profits and larger businesses, and between those who receive state subsidies, like film, and those who do not, such as computer games. Indeed, a vast number of companies are micro businesses (around 90 per cent according to some British estimates), and most do not want to grow but to remain small and therefore flexible and agile. Yet the top few companies can be gigantic, like Comcast or Disney.

After a time lapse, within the European mainland other countries and cities began similar research; and, rather late, the recognition of the importance of the sector was acknowledged by the EU with the first comprehensive assessment of the sector in 2001 called 'Exploitation and Development of the Job Potential in the Cultural Sector in the Age of Digitalisation'.[7] Since then it has become a major focus of the EU. As of 2019 practically every major European city has investigated the potential of its creative industries, and most, such as Amsterdam, Hamburg, Dublin, Zurich, Vienna, Paris or Stockholm, have dedicated

7 https://publications.europa.eu/en/publication-detail/-/publication/e3e9ef3f-3bfc-41a3-9ba6-9f7baaad6doe/language-en.

internal departments or arm's length bodies addressing the potential. Increasingly too the same applies to second and third tier cities, such as Rotterdam, Mannheim, Nantes, Lille or Aarhus.

In 2005 global recognition came when the United Nations Conference on Trade and Development (UNCTAD) set up a high-level panel on creative industries and development and produced its report in 2008.[8]

Two important publications shifted how people interpreted the creative city idea. The first was John Howkins' book *The Creative Economy: How People Make Money from Ideas* published in 2001 (Howkins 2001). It helped push the creative city debate towards the narrower issue of the cultural economy. Howkins made an important contribution, with his central idea being that in the old economy returns start to diminish with the increasing scale of production, as the cost of inputs increases as they become scarcer. In the creative economy there are no limits: endless increasing returns are possible from the production of more ideas and the subsequent innovation that generates more transactions. Howkins suggests that the economy involves transactions in the creative output of the four 'creative industries', namely:

- Copyright Industries: industries that create copyright as their primary product, such as advertising, computer software, photography and film.
- Patent Industries: industries that produce or trade in patents, such as pharmaceuticals, electronics, information technology, industrial design and engineering.
- Trademark Industries: very widespread and diverse creative enterprises that rely on the protection of trademarks and brands.
- Design Industries: very widespread and diverse creative enterprises that rely on individuality in designs.

Subsequently Howkins has taken this work forward in his more recent work *Creative Ecologies: Where Thinking Is a Proper Job* published in 2009 (Howkins 2009). Richard Florida's *The Rise of the Creative Class* came out in 2002, and its slogan 'talent, technology and tolerance' hit the imagination and was very influential (Florida 2002). He argued that a new class of knowledge workers are driving wealth creation in cities and that successful cities needed to attract this group. He stressed that

---

8 https://unctad.org/en/Docs/ditc20082ceroverview_en.pdf.

cities needed a people as well as a business climate, and that a city's success is related to its ability to attract mobile talent and to nurture it. This would then foster technological innovations. To work well, he argued, a city needed to be open to and tolerant of cultural diversity as well as informal and unconventional lifestyles, and to be relaxed about different sexual preferences. This atmosphere is one where there are the arts, good design, a café culture or access to amenities like parks. He proposed a series of indices to measure this atmosphere, the most contentious of which was the 'gay index'. He did not claim they directly caused creativity, but that their greater disposable income helped support the many restaurants and independent shops that make a place vibrant.

Florida's ideas appealed tremendously to urban decision makers across the globe as they sought to reboot both their economies and their cities. It appealed especially to property developers, who tried to create hip, friendly urban neighbourhoods out of declining areas, often leading to gentrification processes.

It did shift the focus of the creative city debate in a different direction. It was contrary to the more grassroots-oriented idea that Comedia and associates had promoted, as it seemed to argue that some special people's creativity is more important than that of ordinary citizens. A slogan we had used was 'ordinary people can make the extra-ordinary happen if given the chance'.

Florida's ideas were increasingly taken up by elites. I am not sure whether Florida could have foreseen this, and since the early 2000s he has revised and clarified his thinking, for instance in *Who's Your City?: How the Creative Economy Is Making Where to Live the Most Important Decision of Your Life* (2008).

In the public understanding the core creative city ideas were often merged with those of Howkins and Florida's rather different conceptions and focus. John Vickery (2017) summarizes this well:

> the original Creative City vision of Landry, et al. has been almost entirely superseded by a Florida-based vision framed by economic innovation and its requisite skilled labour. The Creative City in many places has become a business project, not a framework for total urban policy transformation. . . . It has scaled down its expectations, and no longer demands that urban policy develop a creative imagination. . . . The 'thesis' can be implemented

as strategy without unsettling too many ruling assumptions on the role of cities in the global economic order.

Focusing on the cultural/creative economy sectors was always going to be easier than challenging the complete way a city operates in all its facets. It was not threatening to how cities were run or the political priorities they might take, and seemed to offer economic opportunities.

Unsurprisingly, in the late 1990s and early 2000s the creative industries agenda began to take off globally, and was often called 'creative city'; at various points dozens of cities called themselves 'creative', although their focus was on its economic facets and arts infrastructure, and on the building of cultural institutions.

In 2002 the 'intercultural city' notion was another concept that grew out of the creative city movement. The core idea was to move beyond a multicultural perspective where we acknowledge difference and often keep ourselves separate, to focusing on what can we do together with our differences. It highlighted the potential power of intercultural exchange, sharing, mixing and reciprocal understanding, hybridity and ethnic/cultural difference and how this might help urban creativity and innovation, and the reimagining of citizenship, governance, economic development, cultural activities and public spaces. It saw ethnic and cultural diversity not as problems but as sources of innovation. The notion wanted to move from fixed cultural boundaries to seeing them as in flux. It highlighted cross-fertilization.

The idea was generated from within Comedia, by a group including Jude Bloomfield, Phil Wood, Franco Bianchini, myself and Andy Howell, the then deputy leader of Birmingham City Council. It was a response to the ethnic tensions and riots occurring in Britain in 2001 and 9/11 in New York. In 2002 in Birmingham, Andy asked Comedia to organize a city visioning process called Highbury 3. In that context we invited Leonie Sandercock, the author of *Towards Cosmopolis* (1997), to come to the city as part of our intercultural city project. The 2004 book *Planning for the Intercultural City* by Bloomfield and Bianchini (Bloomfield and Bianchini 2004), triggered by the Birmingham initiative, formed part of a bigger research project, 'The Intercultural City: Making the Most of Diversity', funded by the Joseph Rowntree Foundation and led by Comedia, which culminated in a series of studies in different countries, including Norway, Australia and New Zealand. It resulted in several publications including Richard Brecknock's *More than Just a Bridge* (2006), which explored how planning and designing culturally can contribute to vibrant intercultural cities. The project culminated in *The Intercultural City: Planning for Diversity Advantage* by Wood and Landry in 2008 (Wood and Landry 2008). Phil Wood then became the main advisor to the Council of Europe; he took on the idea and launched the 'Intercultural Cities Network', which as of 2019 has over 100 members across Europe and beyond.

Over the next decade all of these issues – the power of culture, the delights and dilemmas of diversity, the special qualities of the creative economy sectors and urban transformation done creatively – became part of the repertoire of urban development and urbanism. To these were added from the mid-2000s onwards new monikers or labels that proliferated, all of which have relevance to the creative city notion, although their focus, mostly technological, is different. The two most important were 'the digital city' and 'the smart city'. The former is a place where everyone is connected and can easily share information anywhere in the city; it was initially discussed in 1996 when the EU launched a four-year European Digital Cities project (EDC). The purpose was to support European cities and regions deploying new, economically and socially sustainable telematics applications, and to identify related future needs and priorities of local authorities. The latter is the application of high-tech, digital technologies to run cities more effectively, especially through big data and sensors. This idea was launched by Cisco and IBM around 2005.

So we find many labels competing for attention – 'the knowledge city', 'the learning city', 'the intelligent city', 'the information city', 'the digital city', 'the smart city', and increasingly 'the green city', 'the sharing city' and the 'human-centred city'. All are important, yet for me at their source they all require the curiosity, imagination and inventiveness that is the hallmark of the creative city.

References

Andersson, Åke (1987), *Culture, Creativity and Economic Development in a Regional Context*, Strasbourg: Council of Europe.

Australian Local Government Association (ALGA) (1992), 'Making the connections: Towards integrated local area planning: A discussion paper', Canberra.

Aydalot, Phillippe (1986), *Milieux innovateurs en Europe*, Paris: Groupe de recherche européen sur les milieux innovateurs (GREMI).

Bianchini, Franco (2018), 'Reflections on the origins, interpretations and development of the creative city idea', in Ilja Van Damme, Bert De Munck and Andrew Miles (eds), *Cities and Creativity from the Renaissance to the Present*, New York: Routledge, pp. 23–42.

Bloomfield, Jude and Franco Bianchini (2004), *Planning for the Intercultural City*, Stroud, UK: Comedia.

Brecknock, Richard (2006), *More than Just a Bridge*, Stroud, UK: Comedia.

DCMS (2001), *Creative Industries Mapping Document 2001*, 2nd edn, London: Department of Culture, Media and Sport.

Florida, Richard (2002), *The Rise of the Creative Class*, New York: Basic Books.

Florida, Richard (2008), *Who's Your City?: How the Creative Economy Is Making Where to Live the Most Important Decision of Your Life*, New York: Basic Books.

Grodach, Carl (2017), 'Urban cultural policy and creative city making', *Cities*, **68**, 82–91.

Grogan, David and Colin Mercer, with David Engwicht (1995), *The Cultural Planning Handbook: An Essential Australian Guide*, St. Leonards, New South Wales: Allen and Unwin.

Hall, Peter (1998), *Cities in Civilization: Culture, Innovation and Urban Order*, London: Weidenfeld and Nicholson.

Hall, Peter and Charles Landry (1998), *Innovative and Sustainable European Cities*, Luxembourg: European Foundation for Living and Working Conditions.

Hawkes, Jon (2001), *The Fourth Pillar of Sustainability: Culture's Essential Role in Public Planning*, Melbourne: Common Ground, in association with the Cultural Development Network.

Howkins, John (2001), *The Creative Economy: How People Make Money from Ideas*, London: Penguin Books.

Howkins, John (2009), *Creative Ecologies: Where Thinking Is a Proper Job*, St. Lucia, Queensland: Queensland University Press.

Jacobs, Jane (1961), *The Death and Life of Great American Cities*, New York: Random House.

Kennedy, Richard (ed.) (1991), *London: World City Moving into the 21st Century: A Research Project*, London: HMSO.

Landry, Charles (2000), *The Creative City: A Toolkit for Urban Innovators*, London: Earthscan.

Landry, Charles (2006), *The Art of City Making*, London: Routledge.

Landry, Charles and Franco Bianchini (1995), *The Creative City*, London: Demos (in association with Comedia). Available at https://www.demos.co.uk/files/thecreativecity.pdf.

Landry, Charles, Lesley Greene, Francois Matarasso and Franco Bianchini (1996), *The Art of Regeneration: Urban Renewal through Cultural Activity*, Stroud, UK: Comedia.

Landry, Charles, Klaus Kunzmann, Franco Bianchini and Ralph Ebert (1996), *The Creative City in Britain and Germany*, London: Anglo-German Foundation for the Study of Industrial Society.

Matarasso, Francois (1997), *Use or Ornament?: The Social Impact of the Arts*, Stroud, UK: Comedia.

Myerscough, John (1988), *The Economic Importance of the Arts in Britain*, London: Policy Studies Institute.

Myerscough, John, Kate Manton, Ruth Towse and Roger Vaugham (1988), *The Economic Importance of the Arts in Glasgow*, London: Policy Studies Institute.

Robinson, Ken (2001), *Out of Our Minds: Learning to Be Creative*, Oxford: Capstone Publishing.

Sandercock, Leonie (1997), *Towards Cosmopolis: Planning for Multicultural Cities*, Chichester, UK: Wiley.

Scott, Allen J. (2008), 'Resurgent metropolis: Economy, society and urbanization in an interconnected world', *International Journal of Urban and Regional Research*, **32** (3), 548–64.

Törnqvist, Gunnar (1983), 'Creativity and the renewal of regional life', in Anne Buttimer (ed.), *Creativity and Context: A Seminar Report*, Lund Studies in Geography, B. Human Geography, no. 50. Lund: Gleerup Buttimer, pp. 91–112.

Vickery, John (2017), *Creative Cities and Public Cultures: Art, Democracy and Urban Lives*, London: Routledge.

Wood, Phil and Calvin Taylor (2004), 'Big Ideas for a Small Town: the Huddersfield Creative Town Initiative', *Local Economy*, 19 (4), 380–95.

Wood, Phil and Charles Landry (2008), *The Intercultural City: Planning for Diversity Advantage*, London: Earthscan.

Yencken, David (1988), 'The creative city', *Meanjin*, **47** (4).

7   The characteristics of cities

To understand a creative city we need to take a more detailed look at both what a city is and what creativity is, and the dynamics and mindset involved, as only then will we know what can and is to be done. Their manifestations differ through time and place, and now the digitizing age shapes possibilities and dangers in completely new ways.

The smaller context[1]

A city is a complex living organism, a multifaceted and inextricably interwoven entity. It has a history and therefore a culture that reflects its origins and life trajectory; it is a community of people – a society; an economic structure – an economy; a designed environment – a physical artefact; and a natural environment – an ecosystem. They all interact. Together they are planned, managed and governed by an agreed set of political rules and an incentives and regulations regime – a polity.

There are differing types of city and their openness to creative possibilities are often shaped by their geographical setting. A location on inland flats, or a mountainous area, or by the sea shapes the identity and is etched into the DNA of a place. Self-evidently a port city is likely to be more open-minded, as are trading centres given the continuous influx of outsiders and their ideas and different ways of doing things. The dynamic, by contrast, of an inland city with a vast hinterland which it controls, or a mountain enclave, might be more protective. Equally cities that have been invaded often and controlled by foreign interests could develop a suspicious culture. Cities which are religious centres, like a Medina or a Varanasi, may equally be less inclined to experiment and explore than a Yokohama or a New York, or on a smaller scale, an Odessa or a Rotterdam. At times a great history can make once innovative places conservative and complacent as their vigour and verve

---

1   This segment draws on Bianchini and Landry (1994).

declines with their role. Think again here of Florence or Venice, that in their time were pioneering and produced astonishing feats. Of course, what today we would regard as pioneering is completely different.

So the potential for urban vitality and viability needs to encapsulate historic, social, cultural, economic, technological, environmental and political aspects. Creative thinking, especially, sees the interconnections between these different spheres.

Classically there were, and often remain, clear functional areas in differing parts of a city. Typically a typology of zones includes five fairly distinct areas: the city centre; the surrounding – often light industrial – inner city areas; the residential suburbs; the outer residential and industrial areas; and the edge of town. Smaller urban centres such as market towns, some historic towns, seaside resorts, new towns and smaller industrial towns tend to have only three distinct areas – the centre, the suburbs and the edge of town.

Each urban context has identifiable functions and, in principle, creative potential of different kinds, but a big question is whether there is a combined creativity of the parts working together. Yet the low-density and more self-contained private lives of those in living areas mostly constrains, as the spark of innovation often requires proximity. That close interaction can in principle be created in an enclosed tech, science or industrial park where islands of creativity might develop. But the lack of face-to-face interaction, the insufficient diversity of facilities, the high level of homogeneity and the lack of the density of the city core restricts their urbanity – a vital part of a creative ecosystem.

Let us consider the characteristics of these five areas of larger cities, working from the periphery to the centre. Reality is more fine-grained and complex, and there are always exceptions to the rule, but this simple schema, although somewhat clichéd, gives a sense of the relative innovation potential of each area and what its focus could be and what it might entail.

The edge of town has traditionally been dominated by traffic infrastructure, their junctions and motorway entrances, by greenbelt areas and country parks, and by some industrial, logistics, distribution and public utility functions that require easy access for lorries – ranging from industrial parks to water treatment plants and waste dumps. This accessibility makes these areas good for out of town shopping, leisure centres, second-hand car sales rooms and DIY wholesalers, especially located near transport junctions, that compete directly with the city centre so increasingly weakening their economic vigour, which online shopping has exacerbated. Free parking adds to the convenience and so encourages enterprise zones and tech parks.

Being monofunctional they feel lifeless, impersonal and full of tarmac, with dull semi-industrial sheds and inferior architecture – there are no schools, libraries, public administration functions or religious places. There are hardly any places for chance encounters or intimacy; they are not walkable. The elderly, children and those without a car are effectively excluded. Increasingly, however, developers are trying to replicate the urban feel with functions like doctors' surgeries and libraries.

Outer urban areas are mostly residential with peripheral housing estates and swathes of social housing – either low density or high-rise blocks. Mainly built by municipalities to 'decant' working-class families who previously lived in high-density inner urban areas, they can be interspersed with light industrial activities that are usually not high-tech. Increasingly too there are sites for 'cleaner' business parks or shopping sub-centres and leisure facilities, especially in metropolitan areas.

They tend to cluster people on low incomes, there is high unemployment, poor levels of skills and educational qualifications, and low car ownership. Public transport, public spaces, leisure, shopping and cultural facilities are generally bad. The environment tends to be degraded and high in related social problems, ranging from drug addiction to domestic violence and crime, with poor health of the inhabitants linked to diet and lifestyle.

Leisure is predominantly home-based. Youth is often bored and congregates in the streets, often engaging in vandalism or anti-social activities. Criminality can flourish, often under the control of organized gangs – and so does the informal economy. The visual landscape can be dispiriting, and graffiti is everywhere – some good, some expressing anger, some simply ugly. The problems are daunting and interconnected. These places feel forgotten by social service providers, the education system and even the police. Political participation tends to be low and the aspirational searching for social mobility move out as soon as possible, so reinforcing a vicious circle in which these places are trapped.

Within this adversity there can be strength – a strong sense of local identity and community, with networks of self-help, credit unions and community businesses. Innovation is often present in forms of self-expression, especially the arts, such as going with the grain of people's enthusiasms like music making or imaginative self-managed forms of training, and in voluntary activities, focused, for instance, on environmental improvements.

The overall creativity potential of these places, though, is weakened by their monofunctionalism, their physical isolation, the lack of inward investment, the lack of disposable income, their poor image, the fear of crime and the constant leakage of local talent.

The suburbs were developed closely linked with increases in mobility, either public transport or the car. Most suburbs were built to follow transport routes – roads, the metro or railway lines. At times they welded together conurbations of older villages, with their own religious places, pubs, shops, historic houses and other landmarks and facilities. So some suburbs have maintained a local heart with memories of their separate, distinct identities. These often become sub-centres with interesting secondary retailing high streets. Many older, inner suburban areas were historically favoured by professionals. More recently they have become socially heterogeneous with an influx of immigrants or students, as often professionals fled to rural areas. They can be interspersed with facilities, including family hotels or university halls of residence. The outer, newer suburban areas are more socially homogeneous and tend to be favoured by skilled workers and their families.

Income, education and skills levels as well as car ownership tend to be higher. Their convenience makes getting in and out of the city easier. Their own retailing and leisure facilities may be modest, but better than in outer areas. However, people's mobility and being close enough to both city centre and edge of town facilities overcomes this issue.

Yet their 'in between' location can make them characterless and amorphous. There is a local indoor and outdoor public realm, such as cafés, pubs, libraries and squares or parks. Often increasingly they are socially diverse environments with high degrees of mobility common to middle-class families and students. This can mean that it is difficult for stable communities to emerge and the result is atomization and a certain alienation.

Suburban creativity exists, but is often the creativity of individuals, fostered through a supportive environment in terms of schools, money and parental encouragement. Yet, as a spatial entity, suburbs lack sufficient diversity of uses – dominated by housing and overall low density, with few cheap buildings and little land available for creative uses. So, opportunities for face-to-face interaction and collective celebrations are too few for them to become self-generating hubs of creativity, even though typically there are high levels of participation in voluntary activities, although these are mostly driven by older generations.

Inner cities form a ring around the city centre and vary according to the specific history of a place. Mostly there is a mix of decaying elegant residential areas, originally used by the local bourgeoisie; working-class terraced housing, often in proximity to industrial places and ports; public housing, often high rise; amenities created in the late 19th-century period, such as parks, libraries and museums; a variety of worshipping places for different faiths; shopping areas catering mainly for the needs of local communities; and inner ring roads and other traffic infrastructures dissecting them, often created in the post-war period.

Their populations mostly decreased once suburbs were developed, although recently this has been reversing. Today residents typically include some original working-class inhabitants, predominantly Afro-Caribbean, Asian or Middle Eastern immigrants, students and younger professionals, or downsizing baby boomers escaping the suburbs, who want access to urban life. This is leading to gentrifying pressures and enclaves.

Economically you still see small-scale, craft-based industries that have survived economic restructuring by the skin of their teeth yet are struggling. There are pockets of local retailing interspersed with some distinctive, specialist, independent shops, attracted by low rents or universities and educational establishments and a lively 'informal economy' sector.

There is frequently pressure and potential tension in inner cities given the social, economic and racial polarization. The cityscape bears the scars of low-income social groups, unemployment, poverty and social deprivation, with occasional pockets of high earners and gentrification. Such contrasts can result in conflicts and crime.

The creative potential of inner cities is not difficult to glimpse: their strong character; attractive historic buildings and streets; a cosmopolitan and multicultural mix; often interesting shops, that given the associated costs, could not be set up anew in the city centre; the availability of redundant buildings and land for innovative projects, which can be financed through urban regeneration initiatives; the presence of universities or learning establishments; and the large number of students as both consumers and producers for cultural, social and new start-up activities.

Cosmopolitan values are perhaps the main strength of inner city areas. They are expressed in restaurants, street markets, local shops, clubs and manufacturing enterprises, as well as the global networks of those enterprises. Immigrant cultures, when they are open-minded, can bring a diversity dividend with them – their energy, entrepreneurial skills and flair, fresh ideas, challenges and different cultural perspectives can contribute to rethinking how the city works and what it has to offer.

Add to this mix the accessibility of varied city centre facilities and they can clearly be seen as potential creative hubs to reinvent the city as a whole.

The risk is that inner city areas can become closed ghettoes when immigrant cultures are inward-looking and too self-contained, or when one immigrant community is predominant and usually discriminated against by the majority of residents in other parts of the city.

City centres are places where people work, shop, have fun, relax, learn and often live. Working well, they could be the crucial part – the hub, the heart, the engine – of any city, the neutral territory and meeting point for all (traditionally it was the civic centre locating the city hall, the main library or the theatre). When city centres function badly, the city as a whole will not perform effectively. Some structural trends are exacerbating this.

First, land markets and land use are being commercialized, with the weakening of the powers and resources of municipalities. They cannot now bend market forces towards bigger public interest objectives. Planning regimes are not able to protect lower-value but valuable uses, such as independent shops and housing. So city centres are dominated by giant retail chains (approximately 80 per cent in Britain in contrast to 30 per cent in Italy) and office uses, which erode the public realm, leading to a decline in public and social life in the evenings and at weekends. The standardized architectural and design styles tend to make every city centre look the same.

Second, city centres are weakening given the dispersal of office, shopping and public administration functions to off-centre locations that increasingly try to mimic the city centre mix, but with greater convenience. This includes easy parking, more space and space for expansion. Additionally, the dynamic is driven by municipalities' need for cash, and to realize profits they need to sell city centre buildings. This threatens the viability and vitality of city centres.

Third, the loss of population is reducing the city centre mix and the natural surveillance this provides, so exacerbating the problems of relative deadness and lack of safety at night. This is slowly reversing as sheltered housing, student accommodation and fashionable flats for higher-income groups are being built.

Fourth, the dramatic change in retailing driven by online shopping is hollowing out retailing areas, causing many leading department stores or others to close. Shops have to rethink their offer, often trying to become retailing centres. With smaller towns in particular, their high streets are filling up with cafés, hair salons, nail bars and other personal services. Yet often these cannot afford the rents that are frequently set at historic higher prices. The result, especially in weaker places, are large numbers of 'to let' or 'for sale' signs.

In principle this can create potential as underused outlets are being offered to temporary or even longer-term uses, such as co-working spaces where a younger cohort can try out business ideas or where unused shop fronts become galleries that in a normal market would be unaffordable.

Yet overall awareness of the strengths of city centres is growing even though they have to rethink how they represent themselves. They remain the hub for mixing people to cluster skills. This is where most urban communications and transport networks, especially public transport, is based. Most important, railway stations, metro systems and bus networks focus on the city centre, with extensive road systems branching out from there and ultimately linking to major motorways connected to the outside world. A threat is posed by the decentralization to greenfield sites outside the city of key centres for the knowledge industries such as science parks, research institutes and universities. These centres have often developed their own communications networks across the world.

The bigger context

There has been a dramatic shift over the last 30 years in urban form, with the worldwide growth of population a key factor as cities have sprawled into the far horizon as urban expansion spread. Consequently the tight urban boundaries once so crucial are evaporating into metropolitan areas and regions covered by a blanket of 'cityness'. The extreme is the Pearl River Delta with 120 million people covering a vast area of 39 000 sq. km. Greater Tokyo with 33 million people, New York with 20 million and Randstad in the Netherlands constitute a new kind of megalopolis, the last consisting of the four largest Dutch cities – Amsterdam, Rotterdam, Utrecht and the Hague – and a population approaching 8.3 million, but easily connected.

Metropolitanization and the increase in city size are likely to continue inexorably, since when I was born in 1948 there were 2.6 billion people in the world and now there are 7.7 billion – and indeed the climate change implications of this are frightening given the energy use of each individual and the fact that as places develop economically they use more energy.

The intensity of globalization and its dislocations has changed the world's urban hierarchy. Cities of every size in every location face periods of deep transition largely brought about by the vigour of necessary restructuring. The reinvention of some places like the Ruhr area, Bilbao, Helsinki, Melbourne, Chicago, Copenhagen or Vancouver is emblematic of this shift as each city region needs to reassess its role in this new configuration as they need to move their economy to one based on greater knowledge intensity. That grouping, for instance, can be deemed to be creative, and a few, like Helsinki, have been socially inclusive in this shift.

Unavoidably every city region of real ambition wants and needs to *move up the value chain and capture centrality* for themselves. This is why city regions are continuously seeking to be global niche centres of significance. The overall aim of these ambitious places is to *increase their 'drawing power'*, by whatever means. Drawing power assesses the dynamics of attraction, retention and leakage of power, resources and talent. The right blend makes a city attractive and desirable, with different aspects tempting different audiences: power brokers, investors, industrialists, shoppers, tourists, property developers, thought leaders, ordinary people. Overall this creates the resonance of a city. Few places manage to develop the integrated and sophisticated city marketing that brings these elements together. Melbourne, Amsterdam and Berlin do it well. The consequence of achieving drawing power shows itself in economic, political and cultural power – the ability to shape things – and thus performance and wealth. Crucially other dimensions of competition are emerging, such as being 'green', and here places like Zurich, Freiburg and Copenhagen have made a significant impact.

Cities now compete by harnessing every dimension of their asset base, and practically all the major global city region players have recognized 'creativity' as a new, multifaceted resource. Many have creativity strategies, such as Singapore, Amsterdam, Berlin, Shanghai, London, Hong Kong, Osaka or Toronto. Increasingly too, second and third tier cities are following in their wake.

The resources city regions can creatively use can be hard, material, tangible or soft, immaterial, intangible; they can be real and visible or symbolic and invisible; they can be countable, quantifiable and calculable or to do with perceptions and images. Ambitious cities seek to project and orchestrate their assets 'iconically'. The aim is to pull attention to the city, to create a richness of association and recognition, and to grab profile. Icons are projects or initiatives that are powerfully self-explanatory, jolt the imagination, surprise, challenge and raise expectations. You grasp it in one. In time they become instantly recognizable and emblematic. Very few of these exist, and most fail. The newest successful one is the Elbphilharmonie in the HafenCity Hamburg built by Herzog de Meuron, which like many such endeavours has gone vastly over budget. Another is the Calatrava complex in Valencia that has left the city in immense debt. Others that have caught the imagination include the Palm in Dubai and those popping up in the Middle East, like the cluster of museums in Abu Dhabi, including its Louvre. Most memorable icons are physical. An icon, however, can be tangible or intangible: a building, an activity, a tradition, having a headquarters of a key organization in the city, the association of a person with a city, a plan or an event like the Olympics can all be iconic. A city can even be iconic when it has many associations that build upon each other into a powerful composite picture. Most importantly, images and perceptions need to be grounded in reality.

There is a vortex effecting a few cities across the globe. It acts like a vacuum cleaner sucking up the ambitious, the money or the new nomads as well as tourists from everywhere. It is creating a new level of problem both in scale and in kind in European cities like Amsterdam, Berlin, Lisbon and increasingly Athens, in North American cities like New York, San Francisco and Toronto, in South American cities like Buenos Aires and Santiago, and in Asian cities like Shanghai, Beijing and Tokyo. They are popular – perhaps too popular. This is endangering the assets and resources that made them great and so attractive that they are in danger of becoming dysfunctional. Typically they have historic advantages as economic, political or cultural capitals, as well as their heritage and a sophisticated urban texture and activity base to match. These are magnetic places; they resonate and trigger rich associations in the public imagination. They are diverse places.

Steadily, and then suddenly as if in the blink of an eye, the sheer volume of people and projects has swept over these cities and even overwhelmed them like a wave. The 'anytime, anyplace, anywhere' phenomenon – enabled by digitization – is now changing how we interact with space, place and time, whose deeper effects have only just begun. There is excitement and concern in equal measure.

Yet this pressure cooker process has had effects, escalating several wicked problems that are difficult to address within simple free market thinking: the negative effects of gentrification where rising costs push locals into more peripheral areas; the crisis of affordable housing especially for the young, often exacerbated by Airbnb; the takeover of city centres by tourists and travellers; the decline in locally distinctive shops; the dull blandness of chain stores. Others feel overwhelmed by too much diversity. Locals increasingly feel they have lost their city, and the increasingly strong reactions are just a foretaste of what is to come.

There are winners and losers in this global process, and the latter are those vast numbers of shrinking cities whose vitality is draining as their economic purpose erodes; the ambitious leave and they are left often with the less educated. Few cities have sought to reinvent themselves inclusively and to work against the economic dynamic that increases the divides between the rich and poor and reinforces spatial and racial segregation. The Nordic cities are an exception.

The creativity agenda needs to refocus on those shrinking cities, as well as small to medium-sized ones that are not the centre of attention. These in turn need to work out what their assets could be.

This overall dynamic should shape what we mean by being creative, and the main globally agreed agendas are a good starting point; they include the UN's Sustainable Development Goals (SDGs), and especially SDG 11 focused on cities; the New Urban Agenda agreed by UN Habitat III in Quito 2016, which highlights the need to create 'inclusive, safe, sustainable and resilient cities'; the Paris Agreement on Climate Change in 2016; the EU's Urban Agenda; the Sendai Framework for Disaster Risk Reduction 2015–2030; the World Urban Forum 2030 Declaration with its focus on tackling all inequalities and especially 'Encouraging the sharing of creative solutions and innovative practices which enable a shift in mindset necessary to drive change'; the Global Solutions Summit, which provides policy advice to the G20 and which has focused on the need for systemic change and a paradigm shift, especially recoupling social and economic agendas; and finally, the EU's Human Centred City agenda proposed by the Commission that I chaired.

The issues are clear, the agreements are there, but implementation is insufficient, and we know the obstacles: an economic logic that pushes us into unsustainable growth, denial of the problems and entrenched interests that do not want to change. This then focuses us on being ever more determined to decarbonize our cities, on rethinking food systems to shorten food miles, on creating a circular and sharing economy driven by cradle to cradle thinking where waste is also a resource, on being human centred. Some say urban hell and urban delight have always lived side by side. Our love of place and our aversion to it is an ever-present paradox, and never as topical as today with our fears of destroying nature.

Reference

Bianchini, Franco and Charles Landry (1994), 'The Creative City Working Paper 3: Indicators of a Creative City', *A Methodology for Assessing Urban Viability and Vitality*, Stroud, UK: Comedia.

8 The qualities of creativity

Qualities and attributes

Creativity is a general, all-purpose, problem-solving and opportunity-creating capacity. It can be applied to an individual project, creating or renewing an organization or to the development of a city. Its essence is a multifaceted resourcefulness and the ability to assess and find one's way to solutions for intractable, unexpected, unusual problems or circumstances. Equally it helps a process of discovery through the supple capacity to imagine possibilities, to conceive and originate concepts and ideas, to have ambition and a vision and then downstream to help bring that potential into being so enabling it to unfold.

Creativity is applied imagination using qualities like intelligence, inventiveness and reflexive learning along the way. It is valuable in the social, political, organizational, cultural and urban field as well as in technology and the economy. So far creativity has been largely discussed in terms of the arts and sciences, and it is legitimized in those fields. This is fine, and both these fields have unique qualities and important contributions to make in terms of looking at the world afresh or discovering new opportunities or solutions to problems.

Importantly, creativity is not confined to the arts or science and can be applied to all spheres: from rethinking schools and teaching to create more effective learning; to inventing new systems of healthcare and delivery to increase levels of well-being; to addressing climate change; to establishing ways to make the most of diversity; to fostering social innovations; to recasting organizational structures to motivate and empower people and become more efficient; to creating an urban plan that encourages people to meet and mix; to thinking up new business models; to encouraging new innovations that the population might come up with through crowdsourcing. There is thus economic, social, technological and cultural creativity. This means public administrators, urban planners, social workers, businesspeople, teachers or historians can in principle be just as creative as an artist or scientist. It depends on their mindset and how they approach challenges.

Different disciplines have varying attitudes towards being creative, and what creativity is for them will differ. To generalize, for instance, from engineers you want attention to detail and an analytic, logical and systematic approach and the ability to problem solve. From a project manager you want a clear understanding of project objectives, a clear outline of expectations of each person's role in the team, a strong focus on getting results and the ability to cooperate. A social worker should have a strong desire to help others; they should be emotionally mature, objective and sensitive to other people's feelings and accepting of all differences and thus be non-judgemental. You want artists to be less rule bound; you want them to use more imagination, to push you towards greater insights and possibilities. You want them too on occasion, to concern themselves with beauty. From a scientist you want a clear hypothesis and then rigour, clarity and precision. Yet in all these job contexts it is possible to be creative even though in these tasks creativity is not always the primary objective as it is for a designer. The engineer can rethink how a bridge might work, a project manager might invent a new process, a social worker might work with clients in a new way.

Crucially, it is now recognized that creative inputs add value to businesses which are not normally considered creative, such as engineering, facilities management, city development or the hospitality industry, quite apart from fields like design, film or music with which we normally associate creativity. Creativity is both generic, a way of thinking and a mindset, and specific and task oriented in relation to applications in particular fields.

The creative mind

The ability to be creative requires us first to be curious, which is inquisitive exploratory behaviour. Curiosity triggers the imagination – the ability to form images in the mind. These two steps are the ingredients with which it is possible to be creative. Being curious, imaginative and creative are all open processes that explore and create possibilities. This requires physical and organizational environments, settings and management cultures that encourage this to happen. Ideas or projects then have to go through the reality checker to assess whether they are useful, helpful and feasible. Those that are then become inventions. When they are applied they become innovations.

Creativity requires certain qualities of mind, dispositions and attitudes. This applies to individuals, organizations and the city itself. These characteristics include curiosity, openness and a questioning attitude; the ability to stand back, listen and reassess; the courage not to take a given credo, practice or theory for granted and to dare to think outside of the box; the gift of seeing relevance and connections between apparently different things. It involves fluency and flexibility and the ability to draw on ideas from across disciplines and fields of inquiry, to think laterally and to blend concepts from seemingly unrelated domains. It is based on open-minded thinking, which opens out possibilities, reveals patterns and helps find solutions before prematurely closing in on a specific answer.

Creativity is not only concerned with the new or a loose openness. To be effective in being creative means having the judgement and knowing when to be flexible and open and when to be more focused and closed or tenacious and persistent. A misconception is that being creative is about being unconstrained and always searching for the new. Being creative requires just as much attention as being a scientist or an engineer. The central point is that it is a different kind of attentiveness and approach. So in terms of education, as an example, creative learners need four key qualities: to identify new problems, rather than depending on others to define them; to transfer knowledge from one context to another; to treat learning as an incremental process, in which repeated attempts will eventually lead to success; and to pursue a goal. The range of skills required include self-organization, being interdisciplinary and having personal and interpersonal abilities.

Everyone is in principle creative, but not everyone is equally creative, although everyone can be more creative than they currently are. The same applies to organizations, neighbourhoods and city regions. Some aspects of creativity can be learnt, but many individuals or organizations have default ways of thinking. Some flourish in a more free-ranging context, others find it threatening and destabilizing. It seems that most people and organizations prefer the comfort zone of the tried and tested, the known and apparently proven.

Creative behaviour and the ability to innovate mostly occur when two types of mind are present. One is the exploratory, opportunity-seeking and connecting mind that can range horizontally across facts, issues and specialist knowledge and detect threads, themes and cross-cutting agendas. This is the enabling mind associated with being creative. This needs to be allied to the focused, vertical mind of someone who knows a topic, subject or discipline in profound detail. This is the instrumental mind. This is why building teams with diverse skills is crucial. There is a major educational challenge to embed this thinking into learning systems, from schools to university learning.

A creative person has many qualities that we associate with entrepreneurs. They are active agents who organize ideas, possibilities and resources. Indeed, there is as much creativity in having an idea as there is in executing it, that is, creating a new reality and then marketing it. Slightly different competences are required for each step.

I evolved a contrast between the 'urban engineering paradigm' of city development focused on hardware and 'creative city making' which emphasizes how we need to understand the hardware and software simultaneously. Today the essential element of the personality of many cities is their 'culture of engineering' which is reflected in their mentality. The attributes to foster creativity associated with this mindset are both positive and negative. It is logical, rational and technologically adept, it learns by doing, it tends to advance step by step and through trial and error. It is hardware focused. It gets things done. There is a weakness in that this mindset can become narrow, unimaginative and inflexible and forget the software aspect, which is concerned with how a place feels, its capacity to foster interactions and to develop and harness skill and talent. Mindsets either foster or hinder and block creative potential. The challenge therefore is to embed an understanding of the soft and creative thinking into how a city operates. Developing a *'creativity platform'* is a main strategic tool in establishing a comprehensive *'creative ecology'* within a city.

Creativity and innovation

Creativity and innovation are often confused and used interchangeably. This is unwise, although the terms are related. Creativity is the precondition for innovations to occur downstream. There can be no innovation without creativity. Innovation is a positive result of the creative process.

Creativity opens up possibilities; yet generating innovations, by contrast, is a convergent process of sorting, trialling and testing that leads to the successful exploitation of new ideas, products or processes or services. In this process ideas that do not work are thrown out. Public sector innovation is about new ideas that work at creating public value and respond to the public interest. 'The ideas have to be at least in part new (rather than improvements); they have to be taken up (rather than just being good ideas); and they have to be useful' (Mulgan 2008). The concept of 'public value' is used as an analogy to financial value-added in the private sector.

To capture the dynamics of innovation, analysts now stress the interactions and relationships of all actors in a system, such as a city, from firms to universities, civic activists or public agencies. They are thus coming close to the idea of the creative ecology of a place or the creative milieu or environment, which is a place that has created the conditions for people to operate imaginatively. So the creativity and innovation agendas are aligning and connected. This effects how its ecosystem is measured.

Innovation thinking has moved from simply focusing on inputs to a systemic approach. It has become clear that, for instance, levels of research and development expenditure in a firm do not on their own, by definition, involve creativity or lead to innovations. Wider conditions, namely the creative climate or organizational culture, it is recognized, determine the capacity of a place to be innovative within which specific attributes are necessary components, such as good education and skills or research expenditure. Current discussions on innovation indices now include ideas such as 'total innovation' or 'hidden innovation'. This draws attention to how creative thinking needs to pervade a whole environment.

Auditing creativity and innovation together helps us understand the front end and back end of how new ideas are generated then get turned into reality and are adopted and diffused. Understanding how creativity moves through to applied innovations means looking simultaneously at the cultural context and value base of a city, as this determines the extent to which a place can become creative. This wider creative operating environment helps describe the dynamic relationships that influence inventions and innovations and subsequently clusters of activity, how firms operate, the vigour of civic life or its activism and how this collectively shapes the innovating network and its ecosystem as well as the operating conditions of the public institutions. In thinking through innovation it is increasingly clear that the ability to be curious, imaginative or creative is a precursor and precondition to generating an innovation.

In other words, we need to look at how new ideas, processes, social energies, models or technologies are diffused as well as created and what life-long training and learning is required to keep this creative ecology going.

Value and values

Value creation is being reconceived. In parallel with the discussions about creativity, such as 'what is its nature?', 'who is creative?' and 'where is it located?', there have been intense debates within societies and social groups, within business and increasingly within public bureaucracies about the need for and nature of innovation. These conversations do not sufficiently cross over. The innovation debate initially focused on business activities and the private sector. Increasingly we realize this narrow approach is inadequate as cultural or social value and values need to be equally addressed. The complexities we face, such as climate change, the entrenched problems of inequality or the sense of disempowerment people feel, means we need to shift focus to look at issues like power, interests and whether the system itself needs dramatically reassessing.

Focusing first on business, there was the contrast between the 'investment-based competitive stage', where performance depended on the capacity to produce standardized, quality goods and services competitively, and the 'innovation-based competitive stage'. Here the competitive performance idea shifted to spotlighting the capacity to efficiently and sustainably produce innovative goods and services at the technological frontier, clearly with the aim of creating profitable activities. This shift has created an innovation frenzy, especially given the disruptive possibilities of the digital era with big data being a driver. For instance, as of 2019 there are approaching six million apps within the five major app stores – Google Play, Apple Store, Windows Store, Amazon Appstore and Blackberry World. All of these needed to be invented. Then there is artificial intelligence (AI), which will equally generate feverish activity.

Two notions began to predominate. First was the idea of the 'experience economy' (Pine and Gilmore 1999). Here businesses focus on generating value by creating memorable products and orchestrating unforgettable events for their customers, which is the 'experience', and sectors such as film, design, music and new media are central in creating these. The 'creative economy' highlights how money is made out of ideas and how value can be added to all businesses through media, design and performance. The second is how new underlying trends in knowledge capitalism, such as open source innovation, are evolving based on user-driven product development and co-creation. The digitizing world has driven new IT platforms. In addition, web 3.0, with its immersive, interactive, ubiquitous and experiential focus, has exacerbated this shift to co-creation as well as the changing nature of new products and services. It is foreshadowing the development of the so-called fourth industrial revolution. Think of Airbnb, Uber or the social media platforms, such as Facebook, Pinterest, Instagram, Snapchat, Twitter or LinkedIn, with newcomers coming on to the market with increasing frequency. These technologies enabled the 'sharing economy' (Botsam and Rogers 2011) to emerge, from bikes to cars, apartments and even clothes. Here trust has become significant, and as Rachel Botsam notes in *Who Can You Trust?* (2017), 'the currency of the new economy is trust'.

Economies, societies and cultures evolve, and new necessities emerge. We saw the rise of the quality imperative, the notion of the added value of design, the need for continuous innovation and creativity and, more recently, the need to be able to operate in a digital world which has enabled 'smart city' developments (Townsend 2013). They highlight how the conditions to become successful as organizations, cities and regions has changed. Together they form part of a new common sense. They are competitive tools. The aim is to embed their potentials into the genetic code of places, but critically. The current danger is that technologies control us rather than the reverse.

Special attributes explain the significance of each of these guiding ideas, each of which has their version of creativity. Quality requires conscientiousness, attention to detail and the maintenance of high standards as the threshold of necessary 'quality' has risen. It highlights the ideal of *reliability, consistency and predictability* and the concept of continuous improvement and just-in-time production. Total quality management highlights the idea of *alertness, adaptability and responsiveness*. Now it is not simply continuous improvement that is required, but breakthroughs in how people think and solve problems. In the quality paradigm, improvement is regarded as step-by-step or one-dimensional change, while innovation is seen as multidimensional, sometimes involving breakthroughs. Delivering a solution that is unique is becoming more important than delivering a standard solution with near-perfect quality. The quality of design of any resulting innovation becomes the differentiating factor. Design differentiation creates competitive advantage. Design links functionality and aesthetics. It is a bridge to turning creative ideas into innovations. The desire to generate rich experiences made good design a prerequisite for success.

The central question is 'what are we designing or creating in this innovation frenzy?' Is this a design that helps greening or is it frippery? For too long it has been goods and services that drive up unnecessary consumption as firms need to innovate to maintain profitability and to deal with the pressures of global competition. Often they damage the environment and probably do not make us happy. Do we need 20 versions of vodka or 30 varieties of jeans? Another pattern of growth is required where 'cradle to cradle' thinking (Braungart and McDonough 2002) should be at the core of making the world more sustainable.

This reminds us of the need to shift the focus of creativity and to enlarge the scope of desirable innovations beyond product innovation in private companies to include innovations in the public sphere such as in healthcare or social services or new forms of service delivery or governance. The central question remains 'do we need all these technology innovations and are they addressing the right purposes?' This bigger task is to create a fairer world, to decarbonize the economy, to make the sharing economy really sharing and more. One inspiring model is the network of over a hundred Impact Hubs[1] across the world. Their aim is to build socially focused entrepreneurial communities that can have an impact at scale, and they currently have 16 000 members dreaming and innovating to create tangible solutions to the world's most pressing problems.

Scale and scope

Individual, organizational and urban creativity are different, although the general creativity principles outlined above apply to all. We can grasp quite easily what a creative individual might be like; for instance,

---

1 https://impacthub.net/.

their capacity to make interesting connections, to think outside of conventional patterns and to have sparks of insight. They have energy and some sense of where they are going, although it is often unclear how they will get there. The same is true for a creative organization. But already the priorities are different, and it adds a layer of complexity and a different dynamic takes place.

A creative organization probably has mavericks and creative individuals in it, but for the organization to work it needs other types of people too: consolidators, sceptics, solidifiers, balancers, people with people skills. Some people consider them as less interesting, but that is dangerous, because for the creative organization to work it needs mixed teams, a variety of talents and different insights. Indeed, these may come from people with differing cultural backgrounds and thus mindsets. How teams in organizations work together, as well as the organization as a whole, becomes significant. You need to achieve a series of balances, such as between being collaborative internally and perhaps using external competition to push you forward. And the organization needs a story and a proposed trajectory to give itself purpose, in an attempt to make itself more internally cohesive. The task is to align internally to face an outside world. Indeed, it may be the case that a creative organization has quite 'ordinary' people in it, but because its spirit or ethos is open, exploratory and supportive, this maximizes the potential of each individual and how they work together. In this process developing trust between people and parts of the organization is key and leads to greater, sustained organizational achievements. This often happens in sport, where a team with no supremely gifted individuals wins because it knows better how to make the most of its parts. The key is its open ethos. The value of ethos and trust is incalculable.

There are differing organizational types whose criteria for effectiveness and scope for being creative vary. The profit motive still dominates within private companies, yet the range of urgent problems the world faces means many now realize that market-oriented decision making on its own is an impoverished theory to make the world and cities within them better. Some seek to balance social concerns with economic performance. Public organizations, by contrast, focus, or at least they should, on the public interest, where issues of transparency, equity or fairness rise to the fore. Here the goal is to generate public value, and what that is becomes part of the political choice-making process. Civic organizations, in turn, typically act on behalf of social groups, perhaps with a goal to empower or to solve a problem like homelessness. Again the creativity required to solve a problem will differ.

Moving on to the next layer of complexity, namely the creative city, issues become very difficult as complexity rises exponentially as you involve a mass of individuals and a diversity of organizations with different cultures, aims and attitudes, interests or codes of behaviour. These can push in opposing directions. There can be differences in power and influence or resources. The public sector can often appear to be more unified and others more fragmented, like business or the community sector. Aligning these forces so each can give of their best can be complex. For example, it may be that some groups are pushing for urban expansion and extension, whereas others are focusing on the sustainability agenda and want to densify things. Or one organization may display great cultural understanding and help a community cope with change, whereas another may basically not be interested in thinking about softer, more intangible issues even though they are vital. The challenge then is to discover where the lines of strong agreement can flow and to build on these so that similarities become more important than differences, out of which a joint vision can then emerge.

This means that developing partnerships between varied groups becomes key in order to work out a direction of travel for the city or a set of principles by which to progress. You do not want complete agreement on everything as creativity thrives on an element of tension through which new opportunities and solutions emerge because there is discussion, debate and even argument.

Critical mass and size

Creativity potential is determined by its contextual setting. These factors are often beyond the control of a place or city. They include the physical location, the geography, the size of the place, the national politics or the levels of centralization. In relation to Bilbao in Spain, for example, an important challenge is that the world is turning eastwards and facing the Atlantic puts constraint on what is possible. This location means that Bilbao cannot be an entrepôt like Singapore. Second, Bilbao, with a population base of 1.15 million inhabitants and with the rest of the Basque Country at 2.15 million, may be too small to achieve certain things. In assessing creativity, the expectations of a place with a size of 50 000 inhabitants or 250 000 or 500 000 or 1 million or 3 million or 10 million will be different. Critical mass is key in achieving certain aims.

Certain global cities like Paris, New York, Berlin, London, Beijing or Shanghai are magnetic and have an inbuilt advantage. They exert the previously mentioned vortex effect. They attract the highly skilled, resources and opportunity. They are strategic places and hubs which have a direct effect and influence on world affairs economically, culturally and politically, where global agendas are created, facilitated and enacted. There are perhaps 25 cities of this type globally. Here a critical mass is generated as they cluster high-level research institutions, the strategic headquarters of companies, think tanks, stock exchanges and major cultural institutions, and mostly they are the capitals of their country. In particular, they attract cultural creatives and artists. Face-to-face networking opportunities abound, and so a self-reinforcing dynamic evolves and this often gives a push to the start-up culture. That culture has developed as the economic structure has shifted. Whereas large industrial combines and corporations still exist, there is now a growing ecosystem of interacting companies of varying sizes, and especially smaller design or tech entities. What has declined is the vast array of specialized craft businesses.

History can help anchor the position of a place, strengthening its ability to generate critical mass. Cities like London and Paris once dominated the globe as the capitals of their empires, and it was through this that they were able to accumulate resources that enhanced their infrastructures – cultural, political and economic. Their impressive museums, for instance, are full of objects many would say have been plundered from their former colonies. The same applies to New York with its commercial power.

Intensified globalization, in its search for markets, continually collides with cultural barriers. To ease commerce, more seamless transaction points and hubs are needed throughout the globe. These hubs in turn tend to 'control' their hinterlands. Surveying the world, we can think of civilizational zones or realms, although the term is contested as each of these zones is a complex mix of cultures and history and has its own distinctiveness and diversity. There are perhaps ten of these places globally. They are the Chinese, Japanese, Indian, Middle Eastern, African, Hispanic, French, Slavic, English-speaking and American zones. So, for instance, Paris maintains a position despite overall threats for the Francophone world, and Madrid is attempting through an explicit urban strategy to be the centre of the Hispanic world, even though it is a continent apart. Moscow maintains a tight stronghold and hegemony over the Slavic world, while Dubai has attempted to be a focal point for the Arab world and Johannesburg can be deemed the capital of sub-Saharan Africa. While the United States does not fit this pattern well, it is a kind of civilization given its worldviews and predominant cultural attributes. The main point is that certain cities are seen as essential locations and create an allure that attracts. But being too attractive puts stress on infrastructures, as too many people want a share of the city so reducing liveability and the local quality of life. Think here of Amsterdam, where the mass of tourists has become unsustainable. Very large places, especially those without special qualities, often become dysfunctional – think of the booming Chinese or Indian cities and those in South America – and so reduce their creativity potential. Think of the intensity of a Mumbai, Chennai or Delhi, where each has its own form of creativity but the endless traffic, noise, garbage and poverty can deflate. This is no different in the Middle East; for example, Dubai projects itself as on the ball, but its endless traffic jams and controls circumscribes what is possible. Crime, corruption or violence do not help places to be easily creative – think here of Central American countries like Honduras or El Salvador – even though you find incredible people dealing with their daily problems.

Networks and networking

For the first time in history, size and scale can matter less. Aside from those core global cities noted above, large cities no longer have the automatic advantage. This creates opportunities for many second or third tier cities around the globe, if they are globally connected. Networking done well is an accelerator of creative potential. Ghent in Flanders near Brussels is an example; it needs no airport as it can use that of Brussels, and it feeds off its resources. It has a city vision 'to harness all the creative forces in the city to find solutions to difficult problems'. Ghent, for instance, is looking at innovative ways to address growing childhood obesity or to solve issues related to its increasing cultural diversity. Umea near the Arctic in Sweden managed to become European City of Culture in 2014, although few people know about it. It has won several global prizes for public sector innovation. Its university design department redesigned 41 processes of its municipality from a design perspective. This is something very few cities would do. If a smaller city is open, it is often easier to make changes than it is for a larger city.

Size, indeed, can now become a disadvantage, because networking can equally be difficult, transactions too cumbersome and ease of movement constrained. For instance, it is difficult in places like Beijing or Dubai to have more than three meetings in different parts of the city in a day. This is why in world surveys of the best cities places like Copenhagen, Zurich, Stockholm and Vancouver usually come on top. Most have below two million inhabitants. They are walkable, accessible and networked. Even Frankfurt has a population below one million. They are small enough to be intimate yet large enough to be cosmopolitan; even though they may not have the across-the-board strengths, their strong niches can be heard among the din of global information overload.

Anyplace anywhere can become the centre of a universe, whether a tiny niche or something more substantial, as long as it is tenacious and connects, networks and markets itself adroitly and thinks long term. This is the big opportunity for less known cities. We know that in more peripheral cities people with a high level of ambition or talent find it hard to realize their potential. The pool of risk takers and thinking people feels too small to stimulate individuals to achieve more, and this can lead to a leakage of talent and the shrinking cities phenomenon.

A way to overcome talent leakage is to develop and promote very strong niches where localized critical mass can be attained. Within globalized markets, cities can be smaller, but they must be competitive to operate globally. A city can accrue power by *capturing imaginative territory* in the imagination of the world. It can become the central location for an activity, the headquarters of an important entity or be associated with an area that others aspire to. Historically we have had cities associated with gold, such as Arezzo or Pforzheim, or with knives or cutlery, such as Solingen or Sheffield. The task now is to apply those skills to 21st-century contexts and needs.

Corporations capture markets by selling products, much as colonial powers captured physical territories to secure trade routes or raw materials. If cities have few tangible, productive resources, they can capture ideas and networks and get their city to achieve ownership of them. Freiburg has captured a presence as a centre for solar technologies, built on the city's green reputation. By contrast, Milan has a global presence in fashion and design, and Helsinki is within the start-up scene given its Slush Festival, considered the world's largest.[2] Even the

---

2 https://www.slush.org/.

tiny Seaside in Florida has made a name for itself globally in the 'new urbanism' niche, and is the centre of a network.

By assessing the networks in which a city can take a prime position, a city can reflect back to the world some sense of centrality and so attract creative potential. This can be achieved by a concerted effort to join in and participate in relevant international organizations and becoming a focus for meetings. The aim is to capture selective space in the world's imagination. Targeting three thousand international friends of a city is better than having a generalized scattershot approach.

The network idea is emblematic of the age of the 'new economy'. The paradox is that we know networks and networking can make things happen, but often we do not value or sufficiently invest in them because they are not tangible. Neither do the measuring tools we have, such as industrial codes, track how networking might add value.

We have entered a world of almost potentially limitless connection between people, organizations and cities, where constraints of time and place are evaporating. Networking capacity occurs at various levels: between individuals or organizations, between specialist disciplines, city-wide and between cities. The challenge is to translate the known, even clichéd, generic skills of personal networking to the city level.

The words 'networks' and 'networking' have become a mantra imbued largely with positive connotations, as we perceive networking to be about connecting in an open way. Yet networks can have a flip side when they are too tight, closed in or self-referential, only benefiting those who are part of the group. This makes the networking parochial and provincial and can reduce creative capacity. This point comes through in some assessments of Japanese and Chinese creative potential.[3] This issue may emerge more strongly as intercultural creativities, which require connections across cultural axes and networks, become more relevant.

Which cities have global networking strategies in a more comprehensive sense rather than only twinning arrangements or undertaking trade missions? The fact that so few cities have developed these

---

3 See for instance the conclusions of Desmond Hui, *Baseline Study on Hong Kong's Creative Industries*, http://www.info.gov.hk/cpu.

strategies is astonishing. It reveals a lack of understanding of how soft infrastructure works, its role in urban dynamics and what its value is.

Settings and milieu

Creativity needs physical and organizational environments and settings, and a management ethos that encourages it to happen. Many organizations, institutions or cultures inadvertently kill their creativity by crushing their employees, or in the case of education, their pupils' intrinsic motivation – the strong internal desire to do something based on passions and interests. Environments, firms or places that encourage individuals or organizations to become creative have a number of features, including giving people the freedom and authority to act by delegating authority; presenting the right scope of challenge that is achievable but stretches people enough; providing sufficient time and human and financial resources to allow for trial and error as well as to make mistakes; creating a supportive team context where people are committed to the project and to each other, and where ideas and different opinions can be shared to develop the potential of an idea, process or product; and providing managerial and organizational support by creating an environment that publicly values and rewards creativity. Clearly this impacts on how companies, schools, universities, public administrations or city regions operate.

A new organizational ethos is shaping up. It differs from the more simplistic efficiency and effectiveness paradigm associated with the late 20th and early 21st century. The characteristics and operating dynamics of the progressive 21st century corporate structure, civic entity or public bureaucracy include being resourceful, strategically agile, responsive and imaginative as well as being aware of being sustainable and resilient.

The applications of creativity shift with history. In the 19th century it was the creativity of scientists in discovering the cure for cholera that advanced public health. In the 20th century those that invented computers ultimately created the Internet-based economy. In the 21st century creativity is needed to advance the fourth, lean, clean, green industrial revolution, as well as to solve the problems of social integration or conviviality or rethink healthcare and social services. In part this requires people to think differently because then they do things differently and ultimately, perhaps, different things.

References

Botsam, Rachel (2017), *Who Can You Trust?: How Technology Brought Us Together – and Why It Could Drive Us Apart*, London: Penguin Books.

Botsam, Rachel and Roo Rogers (2011), *What's Mine Is Yours: How Collaborative Consumption Is Changing the Way We Live*, London: Harper Collins.

Braungart, Michael and William McDonough (2002), *Cradle to Cradle: Remaking the Way We Make Things*, New York: Farrar, Straus and Giroux.

Mulgan, Geoff (2008), *The Art of Public Strategy: Mobilizing Power and Knowledge for the Common Good*, Oxford: Oxford University Press.

Pine, Joseph and James Gilmore (1999), *The Experience Economy: Work Is Theatre and Every Business a Stage*, Boston, MA: Harvard Business School Press.

Townsend, Anthony M. (2013), *Smart Cities: Big Data, Civic Hackers, and the Quest for a New Utopia*, New York: W.W. Norton and Co.

9   The creative repertoire

The series of concepts emerging in the late 1980s in city making at the origins of the creative city idea always included the word 'culture': cultural resources, cultural mapping, cultural planning, cultural literacy, cultural industries. In addition, the notion of creative quarters gained currency. It felt exciting as a participant. It was as if we were creating a new conceptual landscape. Reflecting back today, I believe the thinking proposed – thinking culturally or a culturally driven approach – has not embedded itself sufficiently into how city development is conducted. One phrase I now realize limited the potential – it is 'cultural planning'. Say that to yourself and what does it conjure up – 'planning for culture'. And this can mostly mean planning for the arts – their institutions, their buildings, their programmes, their events, encouraging artists. Very important, but it does not capture the major shift we were hoping for, which was to think, plan and act culturally. This is seeing culture in its broader sense. 'Planning culturally' would have been better. It is more than word play. It implies that embedding cultural knowledge, insight and understanding in everything done could change the way city making evolves.

Cultural resources

The notion of cultural resources was central to creative city thinking right from the early 1980s onwards. It looks at the texture of life including people's values, beliefs, ideas, activities, tastes and feelings. Cultural resources are ordinary, everyday and diverse, and also sometimes exceptional. Assessing these became increasingly important as the connection between local distinctiveness, the arts and the growth of cultural industries to city development was being made. As urban renewal programmes expanded, there was a concern that standardized models of city building were dominating that were only focused on physical renewal. Programmes were replicated again and again, and cities began to look the same. Equally economic development programmes were insufficiently taking into account the wide range of local potentials. There seemed to be a lack of understanding that the social and cultural domains were a central element of comprehensive regeneration and renewal.

Cultural concerns moved centre stage. People felt there were hidden assets that could be exploited if the authorities took a deeper look. In turn, by acknowledging and going with the flow of local culture, it seemed that neighbourhoods and cities could be energized, and that motivation, confidence and pride could therefore increase. These cultural characteristics in turn shape a city's possibilities for the future. If the culture was inward-looking and parochial, uncovering potentially new resources could broaden the perspective, and if the city had a tradition of being outward-looking, the resources could act as an inspiration.

Cultural resources are the raw materials of the city, and its cultural attitudes represent a city's value base; these resource assets replacing coal, steel or gold. Creativity is the method of exploiting these resources and helping them grow and adapt to the new conditions. The task of urban planners, we argued, is to recognize, manage and exploit these resources responsibly. An appreciation of culture should shape the technicalities of urban planning and development rather than being seen as a marginal add-on to be considered once the important planning questions like housing, transport and land use have been dealt with. So a culturally informed perspective should condition how planning as well as economic development or social affairs should be addressed. Cultural resources reflect where a place is, why it is like it is and where its potential might lead it. This focus draws attention to the distinctive, the unique and the special in any place.

Cities began to look at their unique attributes. Helsinki, often a dark place, saw that its concern for light had a mass of applications and linked its reputation for design to new kinds of lighting. Barcelona used its craft heritage and special aesthetic associated with Gaudi to create a design-led innovation drive. Munich adapted its engineering and science heritage to high-tech products such as cars.

Cultural resources are embodied in people's creativity, skills and talents. The dexterity and knowledge needed to produce, for example, porcelain, fireworks, silk, printing, furniture, lacquer or metal work, products deriving from Chinese culture, can be adapted and incorporated into new innovative products of global relevance. Resources are not only 'things' like buildings, but also symbols, activities and the repertoire of local products in crafts, manufacturing and services, like the intricate skills of violin makers in Cremona in Italy, the wood carvers of the Cracow region in Poland or the makers of ice sculptures in Sapporo or Harbin, an idea that many cities have copied. Every resource, once identified, can also be rethought to generate new products or services. New technologies and digital capacities can adapt and reshape old methods of work and become sources of innovation. Think of how Lyon's textile industry adapted and was able to produce composite materials used to reinforce aerospace structures, such as carbon fibres.

Urban cultural resources include the historical, industrial and artistic heritage representing assets including architecture, urban landscapes or landmarks. They include too local and indigenous traditions of public life, festivals, rituals or stories as well as hobbies and enthusiasms or amateur cultural activities. Resources like language, food and cooking, leisure activities, clothing and sub-cultures are important, as are intellectual traditions or areas of specialized knowledge that exist everywhere but are often neglected, yet can be used to express the specialness of a location and become products that can be sold far afield. Finally, they include the range and quality of skills of the cultural or creative industries.

In Europe, Franco Bianchini played a strong role in promoting and exploring the idea of cultural resources, and his co-authored book *Cultural Policy and Urban Regeneration: The West European Experience* (Bianchini and Parkinson 1994) and another publication, *City Centres, City Cultures: The Role of the Arts in the Revitalisation of Towns and Cities* (Bianchini et al. 1988), were significant at the time.

Cultural mapping

The next step in culturally driven urban development was to detail and map those tangible and quantifiable or intangible and qualitative resources systematically. It is a 360-degree method and tool to identify community strengths and weaknesses in a participative way, giving people and organizations from differing backgrounds and interests a voice to say what values and aspirations they think are important. In pulling this information and knowledge together, the complexity of a city reveals itself, as there will inevitably be differences in intentions and goals. Local community groups may have differing priorities from those of business or public sector institutions, and how to align these potentially starkly conflicting and contrasting worldviews is a central challenge of city making. The challenge then is how planning can use this rich resource to shape urban strategies and in the process overcome the obstacles (Duxbury et al. 2015). The mapping idea seeks to systemize, order and clarify potential. Cultural mapping helps provide an overview and synthesis of the elements of opportunity and obstacles.

The mapping idea built on the work of the multitalented Patrick Geddes (1854–1932), who was rediscovered in terms of the creativity and culture agenda by Colin Mercer (1997, 2009). Geddes was an interesting combination: a biologist and an innovative pioneer of town planning in the early 20th century. In his writings, exhibitions and plans for cities and regions, 'survey before plan' became his rallying cry and maxim, encouraging us to immerse ourselves in the precise details of cities before we act. This is obvious now perhaps, but then it was startlingly novel. His biology background also meant he established some of the key notions of sustainability and regional planning. His writings on *Cities in Evolution* (Geddes 2017), first published in 1915, anticipate by nearly a hundred years our concerns with complexity, the shape of cities and design.

Geddes argued that urban planning was not a physical science, but a human science made up of 'folk, work and place'. Here he attempts to converge the disciplines of anthropology, economics and geography. By 'folk' he meant people. His concern was how people were shaped by their environment and the interactions between what people do and its effect on place. This prefigures too environmental psychology. Mercer notes: 'Geddes' work directly engages with the governance of the "autonomous self" in the form of constituting the *citizen* as a mechanism for establishing a contract between person and environment, individual and society: in *habitus*' (2009; italics in original).

Pierre Bourdieu (1990) was also an inspiration for thinking about cultural mapping, through his notion of 'habitus' and by extending the definition of 'capital'. Habitus is the way social norms guide and entrench behaviour and thinking, and these are constantly both reinforced and challenged by the agency/structure interplay, whereby embedded structures limit and constrain choice and our agency – our ability to act independently – seeks to open out possibilities. Thus, the habitus of a people and place evolves dynamically through time.

Bourdieu describes three forms of capital which are resources. The first is economic, which is the command of assets and money. The second is social; these are the bonds and understandings between people that create shared norms and the unspoken rules and help to develop trust that makes up identity and fosters cooperation. The third is cultural, which is a person's knowledge and intellectual skills, connections and networks that help build status – such as being institutionally recognized, which gives someone social advantages (Bourdieu 1986). These are all forms of power.

Cultural-mapping themes are wide, varied and diverse. It is an asset audit or hunt for potential. It is qualitative and quantitative. It involves *identifying local resources from differing perspectives, be that business, social, technological or cultural. It requires looking at hard and soft factors. It needs various forms of knowledge, be that anthropological, historical, economic or social, and psychological and especially cultural understanding. It means assessing social and power networks and maps of influence in order to get a grip on the dynamics, image and community perceptions of a place.*

Techniques used range from face-to-face interviews to focus groups, surveys, seminars and workshops. The styles of the last two will differ. Often, they feedback interim conclusions and then with the audience jointly develop ideas or co-create initiatives and programmes.

Cultural planning

Cultural mapping turns into cultural planning when the material is assessed. For this to work well requires imaginative, creative and often courageous thinking to make the most of the possibilities. The approach does not just look at needs, but also entrepreneurial opportunities and desires, as well as obstacles and constraints.

Six attributes of the types of thinking required were stressed by Bianchini: first, holistic, flexible, lateral, collaborative, networking focused and interdisciplinary; second, innovation oriented, original and experimental; third, critical, inquiring, challenging and questioning; fourth, people centred, humanistic and non-deterministic; fifth, 'cultured' and informed by critical knowledge of traditions of cultural expression; and lastly, open-ended and non-instrumental. These help build networks of opportunity.

From this a strategy and action plan can be created. David Yencken, one of the organizers of the first Creative City conference in Melbourne in 1988, which focused on the arts and prefigured some of the key themes of the creative city, noted: 'Creative planning is based on the idea of cultural resources and the holistic notion that every problem is merely an opportunity in disguise' (Landry 1998). Thus, every weakness has a potential strength, and even the seemingly 'invisible' can be made into something positive – that is, something can be made out of nothing. These phrases might sound like simplistic sloganeering, but when full-heartedly believed they can be powerful planning and ideas-generating tools.

This reflects what Wolf von Eckhardt said in 1980 in *The Arts and City Planning*, where the English word 'art' is given a much wider meaning well beyond the 'arts' like painting or playing music (von Eckhardt 1980). 'Art' here means doing something well and with thought and quality, such as in the 'art of gardening'. Von Eckhardt said, 'effective cultural planning involves all the arts, the art of urban design, the art of winning community support, the art of transportation planning and mastering the dynamics of community development', to which Bianchini added 'the art of forming partnerships between the public, private and voluntary sectors and ensuring the fair distribution of eco-nomic, social and cultural resources' (Bianchini 1991). I took this con-cept forward in my book *The Art of City Making* (Landry 2006).

Cultural literacy was the fourth element of the conceptual quartet. It is a necessary, vital skill as important as numeracy, normal literacy or understanding the laws of physics, especially now that cities are far more diverse. Without it we wander as if we had no sight or language. Cultural literacy is the ability to read, understand, find significance in, evaluate, compare and decode the local cultures in a place. This allows one to work out what is meaningful and significant to the people who live there. It helps one to understand better how local identity is made up, and what its potential and problems are and how these may be addressed.

All bigger cities are much more diverse in their make-up. Multi-culturalism as a planning concept and a policy is the predominant approach and acknowledges these differences. It highlights the need to cater to diverse needs. Interculturalism goes one step further and has different aims and priorities. It asks instead 'what when we are sharing a city can we do together across our cultural differences?' It recognises difference, yet seeks out similarities. It highlights that in reality most of us, when we look deep, are hybrids, and so downplays ideas of purity. It stresses that there is one single and diverse public sphere and it resources the places where cultures meet. It focuses less on resourcing projects and institutions that can act as gatekeepers, and instead encourages bridge-builders. In so doing it does not consider that there is a cosy togetherness. It acknowledges the conflicts and tries to embrace, manage and negotiate a way through them based on an agreed set of guidelines of how to live together in our diversity and difference.

In sum, it goes beyond a notion of equal opportunities and respect for existing cultural differences in order to achieve the pluralist transformation of public space, institutions and our civic culture.

Cultural industries

Cites took to the idea of the cultural industries very strongly once there was an evidence base that showed they were important. They offered jobs and hope and so it was easier to move forward instead of thinking about the bigger creative city agenda.

Initially the sectors now called the creative economy were called the cultural industries, and there have been many arguments about the definition of the sector and its name. At its core there were three main domains: the media and entertainment industries, the arts and cultural heritage, and creative business-to-business services. So is it the cultural industries, creative industries or creative economy? I personally preferred Enzensberger's (1974) 'Industries of the Imagination'.

Yet a central question was always lurking in the background. Are we talking about a defined number of sectors deemed creative – the creative economy – or are we discussing *creativity in the economy*? To define only certain sectors as creative can make others outside of those feel reduced when self-evidently certain businesses, social enterprises or scientific fields live by their capacity to be creative.

The consensus that has emerged and become dominant is that the creative economy is a platform for developing both the economy and, even, the city, since it can add value to every product or service. Design, advertising and entertainment acted as drivers of innovation in the broader economy and have shaped the so-called experience economy. Negatively, those activities can be used merely to spectacularize the city, with artists increasingly used as the handmaidens to provide the imagination.

There is, however, a deeper transformative effect of the connection between culture and the economy on the individual, the organization, the city and society as a whole, as Jason Potts and Stuart Cunningham (2008) and I have highlighted. The major contribution and impact may be less the actual numbers of people employed in specific sectors like music or design, and more the innovative organizational and production culture that these sectors have fostered.

The historic production methods of activities like theatre, with their emphasis on task-oriented projects, teamwork and changing casts, have found their way into mainstream industry as well, and the now more dominant co-creation processes have affected the overall nature of the economy itself. These have begun to migrate into all economic realms. The creative industries contribute, therefore, not just to adding economic value and jobs, but more importantly to the evolutionary process by which the economic system grows as a whole. For example, design consciousness and thinking is now apparent across industry and services, as is the desire to generate more experientially rich and interactive products that draw on the imagination- and performance-based industries like music or the moving image.

Remember too that behind music lies sound and vibration; behind the painting arts, visualization; behind film, moving images; and that design is in essence a moulding, patterning and problem-solving activity and the new media are largely focused on connections. This under-explored insight is that these attributes and qualities too have migrated into every sphere of life and every industry and service. Think here of medicine, logistics tracking or mining. The creative economy sectors then become the platform through which practically any form of innovation can be generated. This makes their combined impact as powerful as electricity. The current economy could not run without them and they have transformed the way individuals, the city, the economy and society operate.

This drive to create rich sensory environments in cities provides new opportunities for those working in the creative professions. Equally, as the marketing proportion of a product's sale value has increased through time, the scope of work for these professions rises. But a dilemma emerges as the logic of arts and culture can be diametrically opposed to economic rationalism.

Using creativity, culture, the arts and creative industries in city development should not happen formulaically. It is more an art than a science, but strong principles can help cities on their way. These include going with the grain of local culture rather than against it, focusing on the distinctiveness of place and involving citizens in an act of co-creation in making and shaping their evolving city.

A vast array of evidence documents the contribution of this sector to employment and income for urban economies. In addition, the creative industries have softer indirect spin-offs for cities, such as encouraging tourism, increasing their vitality, or shaping their identity.

Creative places

In using the conceptual framework outlined and applying it to a city and its planning, it became rapidly clear that creativity was clustered in certain places, even though the wider aim was for the city as a whole to become and be seen as creative. This then drew attention to where this imagination was being expressed, and it became clear that a creative place can be a building, a street, a quarter, a neighbourhood, a university campus, a tech hub and, very rarely, a city as a whole. So even a building can be a microcosm of a creative place, like the Cable Factory in Helsinki or the Creative Factory in Rotterdam, especially when some of the activities spill out beyond the building itself – indeed, this is more frequently the case.

Three things were required simultaneously. First, to shift the overall mindset in city decision-making circles to be open enough to encourage and to legitimize the enabling conditions to be imaginative. Second, to act – and this was always easier in specific projects, physical developments or places. The notion of creative quarters became popular, but initially these were rather limited in that any cluster of museums or art galleries was deemed to be one, such as the grouping around the Rijksmuseum in Amsterdam, the Museumsufer in Frankfurt, the

MuseumsQuartier in Vienna, or Rue Saint Honoré, the fashion street in Paris. However, these were all places to consume culture rather than to make culture.

Lastly, clustering is key – especially spatial clusters of activities or concentrations of an industry, such as design, biotech or education. The arguments for clustering are well known: mutual financial, technical and psychological support, bringing together buyers and sellers, so increasing efficiency, creating overlaps between adjacent disciplines or accessible centres of excellence and fruitful competition, so generating multiplier effects, synergy, complementary interchanges and swapping of resources. Clustering is not new – the convenience it creates has been obvious since trading began. With real and virtual worlds coalescing, the spatial geography of creativity and clustering is changing, but crucially face-to-face contact remains key. More recently there has arisen socially driven clusters like the Centre for Social Innovation founded by Tonya Surman in Toronto and replicated elsewhere.

Traditionally, it was thought that innovative milieux, especially in relation to research centres or firms, were in enclosed settings (like a university campus) that were often far away from city centres and had little contact with their surrounding urban environment.

In time, focus shifted to thinking of places with an overall atmosphere that reflected urbanity – the personality associated with city dwellers who live the complexities, dense interactions and experiences or perspectives of urban life. It was clear that those creative places were ones where diverse people and organizations were exploring, creating and innovating. These places include all their associated needs, such as ancillary suppliers, workshops, distribution companies and meeting places as well as showcasing opportunities.

To create interesting products and services either driven by craft skills or high-tech possibilities often requires living side by side with people who have routine technical skills, such as in woodworking, welding or lighting. That environment then typically encourages all the additional facilities such as eating places, cafés and potentially entertainment venues from theatres to nightclubs.

This was a common repertoire and was creative in an 'ordinary', everyday sense – people just getting on with their lives. Often the creative quarter would be anchored around one or a few revitalized older buildings – often formerly industrial with many open spaces. These could easily be chopped up into varying sizes where smaller companies, which were often a mix of design, new media and artists' groups, could cluster. This is why such quarters were often based in formerly light industrial areas just outside the urban core rather than spread throughout a city. Indeed, artists were frequently the catalyst for such developments, especially in more degraded areas. The vibrancy later typically attracted a different demographic, such as professionals whose presence encouraged more upscale housing nearby, making the area more likely to gentrify and to push out low-cost uses.

What gave such quarters an added resonance and exceptional quality was their ability to be associated with a sector, ideally cutting edge, that allowed them to stand out from the crowd. Here a new-build cultural facility often also helped. The key qualities of a successful creative quarter are to do with both hard and soft infrastructure; they include a place associated with a guiding set of ideas that can represent a broader movement in thinking and innovation, such as the Sohos in London or New York or Silicon Valley; having some memorable physical qualities and activities that visibly communicate, such as the Marais in Paris; a location large enough to generate impact and critical mass, but also appropriately dense; an overall atmosphere that creates a multi-layered experience, including combining the intimate and the iconic, the somewhat shabby, and the clean and potentially sanitized new; an environment that feels open, diverse and mixed, where the presence of different cultures and people finds expression in the built form and facilities from restaurants to cultural centres; being somewhere that is not too self-consciously orchestrated and planned, so it allows unpretentious authenticity to develop and come through.

In addition, a successful quarter needs a variety of structures for work and living at different price ranges, to ensure start-ups and young innovators have a place to live and work as well as established companies. Interspersing this fabric should be places where non-governmental organizations (NGOs) are housed or community centres. It needs many people too who have lived there a long time, longer-term residents who might have lived there for generations, people who do ordinary jobs from bus drivers to office workers or cleaners – and indeed those jobs can also have imaginative elements to them.

The overall physical setting is crucial in that it should combine the high quality, ordinary and small with the occasional extraordinary gesture and a good mix of facilities which provide the ability to work, to research, to live, to recreate and to relax. Interweaving and blending the old fabric and heritage with the challenging new triggers the imagination, as does having buildings with flexible structures that provide for a variety of uses to ensure adaptability is maintained. Within this certain street patterns inspire, such as those which are intimate, diverse and not dominated by well-known brands and chains, and with built structures from different historical periods. It is the human-scale developments that encourage interaction and mixing, as well as a diversity of third spaces that are accessible for chance encounters, talking, eating and relaxing.

A series of balances need to be maintained, including between production facilities and consumption opportunities; or combining the idea of fostering innovation and nurturing tradition; or ensuring there is a lively mainstream as well as alternative scene and, if necessary, providing grants for the latter; or making sure the place is not overwhelmed by too many tourists or visitors, who can destroy a creative milieu. Furthermore, it should enable the full value chain to be present, from encouraging ideas generation possibilities, to having learning institutions as well as having production facilities and outlets to consume and experience what the creative environment offers. This place should combine commercial and non-commercial activities and uses, such as research centres, not-for-profits, cultural facilities and low-cost subsidized spaces.

Even though much of the animation and activation is self-generated and involves local participation by those living and working there, some curation is necessary. Here, playfulness – and humour especially – generates interest and surprise, for instance through pop-up events or temporary installations.

This all requires a public management structure, perhaps a public–private partnership, that is alert and can ensure that a fine balance is maintained in the area between gentrifying and remaining accessible in terms of cost and cultures. Finally, successful quarters ensure there is the right balance between 'local buzz' and global pipelines.

What constitutes a creative place? Ultimately it is a somewhere where everyone can play their part in shaping, making and co-creating a place of possibility, whether they are a bureaucrat, a social worker, a business person, a planner, a software engineer, an artist or film-maker, or the owner of the local café. It is a good mix of ordinary and extraordinary people. Some are ambitious, hard-working, talented, skilled, and it is their critical mass and the support infrastructures that determine a creative milieu. This can develop a culture of creativity.

Going global

International competitions, events and networks became an increasing part of the repertoire, of which the European City of Culture competition, conceived by Melina Mercouri, then Greece's minister of culture, and Jack Lang, her French counterpart, is the most well-known. Launched in Athens in 1985, it began over the years to have an impact. Initially its aim was to bring Europeans closer together, raise awareness about Europe's common history and values and to show its rich diversity. By bringing the various aspects of culture in a city together – such as the more participatory and high culture – in an extended year-long programme, it helped establish a city's projected cultural vision for itself. The possibility of winning the designation created focus and helped cities form and develop strong partnership working. Many of these partnerships fell away after the year.[1]

All the major European capitals bar London and Rome have been designated, and as the success of the initiative has continued, secondary cities have increasingly held the title.[2] This accolade, conceived and organized well, was and remains an opportunity that can be catalytic in creating cultural, economic and social benefits. It can be vital in changing the self-confidence and the external perception of a place. Other continents copied the idea, such as the American Capital of Culture launched in 2002 and the Arab Capital of Culture scheme in 2002.

UNESCO's Creative Cities Network (UCCN) founded in 2004, that has steadily increased to 180 members and whose *raison d'être* is to celebrate contemporary manifestations of creativity, is another initiative worthy of mention. It is focused on seven fields: literature, music, design, film, crafts and folk art, gastronomy and media arts. Inexplicitly it leaves out the visual and performance arts. Within the network there is an ongoing discussion about whether it is merely art forms that are

---

1   *The Palmer Report on the Capitals of Culture from 1995–2004*, https://ec.europa.eu/programmes/creative-europe/document-library/capitals-culture-palmer-report_en.

2   https://en.wikipedia.org/wiki/European_Capital_of_Culture.

creative or whether cities should be trying to be more comprehensively creative. Here especially the Italian cities who are members – including Torino, Milan, Rome, Parma and Fabriano – favour the latter.

The network is a good idea as UNESCO has status and convening power, but there are a series of fault lines that make its success more difficult to achieve. UNESCO is a global, politically shaped entity. This determines its organizational culture and modes of operating as political exigencies are ever present. Equally, dealing with nation states shapes the thinking and modus operandi. Cities and creative projects within them are inevitably more distant. City leaderships are more pragmatic. They need to solve problems and they need to deliver. This is why they like projects. Can a global bureaucracy run a creativity network, remembering how different this is from overseeing a heritage designation, one of UNESCO's main roles as the entity nominating world heritage sites?

The network is the institution of our time and its dynamics are changing, driven by social media potential and digitization. In a digitized world the more hierarchical, formal institutional networks like those of UNESCO are suffering and seen as cumbersome and unwieldy compared to the quicker world of social media-savvy creatives who thrive more on fluid structures, codes of behaviour and quick responses. When old and new networking worlds clash as in UCCN, this changes the internal dynamics and puts pressure on the balance of power between the network itself, its nodes, the cities involved and the creative projects.[3]

There is a need to bridge the gap between the formal world and the necessities of government and the world of creatives who want the enabling conditions for them to act with greater fluidity. A *more arm's length arrangement* would have been the best way for all parties to give of their best.

The meme replicates

Countries across the world had learnt from the strategies and experience adopted in more developed countries in Europe. One of the

---

3 http://charleslandry.com/panel/wp-content/uploads/downloads/2017/07/Maximizing-the-Potential-of-the-UNESCO-Creative-Cities-Network.pdf.

earliest was in South Africa where in 1998 a cultural strategy group was formed that investigated the potential of the music, film and TV, publishing and craft industries as drivers for the country's development.[4] It resulted in a national policy called: Creative South Africa: A strategy for realising the potential of the Cultural Industries.

Another early national project was supported by Pro Helvetia, the Swiss cultural funding body, in Albania. They felt the broader creative city idea could be taken up in less favourable places like in Albania. In a three-year project from 2004-2006 I sought to help ten smaller places, like Shkodra or Pogradec, think through and implement imaginative ideas to foster both a sense of identity as well as to regenerate difficult areas. Other cultural development agencies, such as the British Council or the German Goethe Institute, also began to support projects from the early 2000s onwards.

Most initiatives elsewhere that developed were focused on the cultural/creative industries. Canada was an early adopter, and already in 2002 had established the Creative City Network in Canada (CCNC), which aimed to address the need to provide support for professionals in the field by tapping into the expertise of differing municipalities across the country.

In China and Korea, especially, the elements of the creative/cultural strategies taken up focused largely on their economic potential rather than on how their overall culture or their city making could change. By contrast specific cities like Buenos Aires took a different approach. From 2004 onwards creativity was seen as a key element in their economic and social development and part of a broader regeneration plan to boost strategic sectors in clustered geographical zones as well as to empower people.

Korea, for instance, made a radical departure in the early 2000s when the government shifted its cultural industry policy from wanting to control creative industries politically to seeing them as a vital cog in its export-focused economic development strategy. This included too substantial government investment in related strategic industries, such as IT. The rise of K-Pop, that had originated in the 1990s, took a leap in the early 2000s as part of the Korean Wave which saw Korean prod-

---

4 This group included Carole Steinberg, Stephen Sacks, Avril Joffe, Stephen Hodes and myself. https://www.gov.za/sites/default/files/gcis_document/201409/ms01bao.pdf.

ucts globalizing. The song Gangnam Style and its dance by Psy, which refers to the lifestyle linked to Seoul's Gangnam district and went viral in 2012, was one catalyst for the West to start buying Korean cultural products, but Korean cultural products were from early on popular in China. Another, more corporate district, Sangam-dong, that began to be opened in 2002, is sometimes referred to the as 'the heart of the Korean Wave'. This Digital Media City is the high-tech centre of Korea's entertainment and digital content industry. By 2013, President Park Geun-hye had announced a plan to move Korea towards a creative economy rather than being a catch-up economy. He stated that the new phase had to generate innovation and foster entrepreneurship.

A similar process is happening in China. From 2001 it began thinking about the cultural industries, specifically calling them 'cultural' rather than creative. They understood the crucial role of culture in generating soft power and influence – a consistent theme since. By 2009, with the 'Cultural Industry Promoting Plan', the sector had achieved a higher status, and in 2011 the government focused on it as a national strategic industry. Like Korea, China was shifting from copying to creating.

Within this strategy Beijing and Shanghai were leaders in revitalizing old factories. Beijing, having all but demolished and erased their hutongs, the narrow alleyways of traditional residential areas, to be replaced by wide boulevards and high-rise apartments, belatedly began to protect the last few. Equally the vast factory complexes were then finally identified as resources to reinvigorate land resources and to enhance the cultural atmosphere of the city. The most famous of these is the 148-acre (0.6 sq. km) 798 Arts District, a decommissioned military factory built in the 1850s in a Bauhaus-inspired style. By 2003 it had become the favoured location for avantgarde artists. Others more recently created and authorized by the Beijing government are the No. 77 Back Street, formerly an offset printing factory turned into a theatre complex, and the Lang Yuan Vintage creative park in Chaoyang district, which now houses enterprises with around 4000 employees, mainly in the creative sectors. These are now some of the most popular destinations in the city. The city leadership has made the protection and utilization of old factories a strategy to expand space for cultural development and creative industries, as well as for public facilities.

In Shanghai the same process is occurring, with the city investing heavily in the creative and design industry, and as a result, there are now over two-hundred creative hubs scattered around the city, including

1933 Shanghai, the astonishing art deco abattoir turned into a hub; M50, the arts district bedded into an area of restored factories; *and* the 800 Show Creative Park, formerly an electrical machine plant. Another is The Bridge 8 complex, which has been turned into a fashion showcase in the centre of the city. In all the Chinese cases these vast complexes are *mostly* self-contained, and their atmosphere does not spread out into the surrounding urban environment.

The Japanese trajectory was somewhat different,[5] and in the early 2000s various cities, especially Yokohama and Kanazawa, adopted a full creative city strategy that, while focused on the modern creative economy sectors, also looked at craft-driven ones, from pottery to lacquer work and origami, acknowledging their astonishing skills. The work of Masayuki Sasaki, who worked with me, was important here, as was his book in Japan, *The Challenge for the Creative City* (2001). The Agency for Cultural Affairs of the Japanese government inaugurated a Cultural Creative Cities Network in 2004 to promote Japanese products, and in 2010 the Ministry of Economy, Trade and Industry (METI) introduced its 'Cool Japan Strategy' to market culturally creative products such as manga and animation. In 2013 the Creative City Network of Japan (CCNJ) was established to act as a platform to promote cooperation and exchange among creative cities in Japan and from across the world, in order to spread the ideas of creative cities in Japan.[6]

With growing intensity the European Commission focused on the creative economy, especially after an important research report titled *Economy of Culture in Europe,* which assessed the economic and social importance of the culture sector for the first time at EU level, was prepared for the Commission in 2006.[7] A major commitment was its Creative Europe programme for the years 2014–2020. This had a budget of €1.46 billion. More recently, in 2017 the EU established the Cultural and Creative Cities (C3) Monitor, a new tool to monitor and assess the performance of 'Cultural and Creative Cities' in Europe vis-à-vis their peers using both quantitative and qualitative data.[8] This first edition covered 168 cities in 30 European countries (the EU-28 with Norway and Switzerland). They assess three dimensions. First, cultural vibrancy measured by the number of facilities and levels of participa-

---

5 http://www.grips.ac.jp/r-center/wp-content/uploads/14-04.pdf.

6 https://www.japan.uni-muenchen.de/download/wise0910/ccc/presentations/sasaki.pdf.

7 http://www.keanet.eu/wp-content/uploads/Final-report-Creative-Value-Chains.pdf.

8 https://www.politico.eu/wp-content/uploads/2017/07/CulturalCreativeCitiesIndex.pdf.

tion. Second, the strengths of the creative economy in terms of jobs. And lastly, the enabling environment, such as human capital and education, openness and trust as well as the quality of governance. Paris, Copenhagen, Edinburgh and Eindhoven take the top spots within their various population categories. It is a rich source of information even though we can argue about some of its conclusions, as London, for instance, does not feature in the top five of cities with a population over one million in Europe. Clearly London is a global cultural leader, and it has initiated the network called the World Cities Culture Forum, which seeks to put the importance of the culture sector centre stage in city development.[9]

Another international institution increasingly involved in the creative economy agenda is the Inter-American Development Bank, which in 2013 supported its version of the creative economy which it called 'The Orange Economy'.[10] It is now being rolled out in South America, starting with Columbia. In 2019 the World Bank and UNESCO agreed a joint position paper 'Culture in city reconstruction and recovery'. Called the CURE Framework, it acknowledges that a different approach to city development is required given rapid urbanization and escalating crises, putting culture at its heart.[11]

References

Bianchini, Franco (1991), 'Urban renaissance? The arts and the urban regeneration process', in Susanne Macgregor and Ben Pimlott (eds), *Tackling the Inner Cities*, Oxford: Clarendon Press, pp. 215–50.

Bianchini, Franco, Mark Fisher, John Montgomery and Ken Worpole (1988), *City Centres, City Cultures: The Role of the Arts in the Revitalisation of Towns and Cities*, Manchester: CLES.

Bianchini, Franco and Michael Parkinson (1994), *Cultural Policy and Urban Regeneration: The West European Experience*, Manchester: Manchester University Press.

Bourdieu, Pierre (1986), '*The forms of capital*', in John G. Richardson (ed.), *Handbook of Theory and Research for the Sociology of Education*, New York: Greenwood Press, pp. 241–58.

---

9 http://www.worldcitiescultureforum.com/publications.

10 Buitrago Restrepo, Felipe and Iván Duque Márquez (2013), *The Orange Economy: An Infinite Opportunity*, Washington, DC: Inter-American Development Bank, https://publications.iadb.org/en/orange-economy-infinite-opportunity.

11 https://openknowledge.worldbank.org/handle/10986/30733.

Bourdieu, Pierre (1990), *In Other Words: Essays towards a Reflexive Sociology*, Stanford, CA: Stanford University Press.

Duxbury, Nancy, W.F. Garrett-Petts and David MacLennan (eds) (2015), *Cultural Mapping as Cultural Inquiry*, London: Routledge.

Enzensberger, Hans Magnus (1974), *The Consciousness Industry: On Literature, Politics and the Media*, New York: Seabury Press.

Geddes, Patrick (2017), *Cities in Evolution*, USA: Andesite Press.

Landry, Charles (1998), *Helsinki, towards a Creative City: Seizing the Opportunity and Maximising Potential*, Helsinki: City of Helsinki Urban Facts.

Landry, Charles (2006), *The Art of City Making*, London: Routledge.

Mercer, Colin (1997), 'Geographics for the present: Patrick Geddes, urban planning and the human sciences', *Economy and Society*, **26** (2), 211–23.

Mercer, Colin (2009), 'Convergence, creative industries and civil society', *Culture Unbound: Journal of Current Cultural Research*, **1**, 179–204. Available at http://www.cultureunbound.ep.liu.se/v1/a11/cu09v1a11.pdf.

Potts, Jason and Stuart Cunningham (2008), 'Four models of the creative industries', *International Journal of Cultural Policy*, **14** (3), 233–47.

Sasaki, Masayuki (2001), *The Challenge for the Creative City*, Tokyo: Iwanami Shoten.

von Eckhardt, Wolf (1980), 'Synopsis', in Robert Porter (ed.), *The Arts and City Planning*, New York: American Council for the Arts.

10 The regeneration repertoire

These overall notions and the overeager focus on the economic opportunity of cultural development challenged traditional arguments of the age of classic culture, whose highpoint was from 1945 to 1979. Here public debate about the arts in Western societies focused on a limited range of cultural activity deemed to require and be worthy of subsidy. 'Culture' had been completely divorced from broader economic concerns, while many aspects of culture, such as film, pop music, photography and the bulk of publishing, were ignored by the arts policy-makers. In many respects, 19th-century definitions of 'culture' shaped the debate. The main rationale for implementing urban cultural policies was their perceived value in re-educating and civilizing people after the horrors of the war, with a strong bias against the uncomfortable and contaminating forces of commercial popular culture and towards the well-established canons of pre-electronic (19th-century) 'high' culture. The prevailing attitude towards 'culture' was a continuation of the 19th- and early 20th-century tradition, which largely viewed appreciation of the classics in the arts as an antidote to the spiritual and even environmental damage wrought by industrialization.

Unproblematically it assumed that the culture in which people participated, effectively the recognized high art forms, was a pre-prescribed unified canon, inherited and given, on which they would not leave their mark or shape. There was a conception of a homogeneous, national culture, handed down to 'ordinary people' by elites. This has since been radically challenged by the diversity agenda, where such unified notions of culture, identity and belonging are seen not to reflect the lived world of many. Cultural managers during this historical phase tended to have more of a curatorial than a developmental role. They tended to be experts with specialist, scholarly knowledge.

Urban cultural policies, as a result, were primarily focused on creating, expanding and subsidizing an infrastructure of traditional, building-based arts institutions located in city centres, such as opera houses, museums and civic theatres. This partly left a difficult legacy of physical infrastructure that needed to be maintained, but also buildings perhaps not fit for contemporary purposes, where more flexible spaces and uses were required. Independent organizations were less funded. Additionally, culture in suburban areas was neglected, and rarely were there facilities there. This has been a long-running sore.

The economic turn, while acknowledging the importance of new cultural forms like pop music, nevertheless in practical terms largely aligned itself with the cultural flagship strategy. One approach within this was to create iconic buildings, the most famous of which was the Guggenheim in Bilbao. Most other examples did not live up to their iconic promise. Mostly from the 1980s onwards, the attention of urban strategists was on the outside visitor, until criticisms forcefully re-emerged that this was too focused on narrow audiences, elites or property interests.

Pulling the threads together, we can detect a repertoire: revaluing the existing cultural fabric; launching new physical interventions, especially cultural facilities; encouraging activity programmes; inventing high-profile events; and refurbishing older industrial structures. Typically, for a period, cities would seek to build or rebuild a contemporary arts gallery, a museum (ideally with a wider content range than the merely local), a concert hall, and often too an opera house and perhaps a major sports facility. Think here of places as diverse as Frankfurt, Helsinki, Bilbao, Rotterdam, Glasgow, Vienna and Valencia, or equally, Melbourne, Sydney, Tokyo, San Francisco, Miami or Toronto of the larger cities.

One of the legacies of these policies is that maintenance costs and loan charges were often so high that they absorbed most of the resources available for programming, leaving us often with beautiful containers without content. There was a tendency in times of financial stringency to curtail revenue funding for those activities seen as 'marginal' – often those aimed at disadvantaged social groups, or those that were innovative and experimental in character – rather than to withdraw money invested in theatres, concert halls and other building-based, traditional arts institutions.

Three trends lived side by side: classic ways of developing culture, economically driven cultural development and the participatory approach. The vigour of the 'age of participation' in the 1970s and early 1980s had become too uncomfortable for many involved in regeneration. It challenged the classic model of urban cultural policy-making, given the interconnected changes exemplified best by the events of May 1968 in Paris as well as Rome, Berlin and London. Think here of the post-1968 emergence of grassroots and social movements, such as feminism, community action, environmentalism, youth revolts, LGBT+ and ethnic minority activism. The last in this list, LGBT+ and ethnic minority activism, prefigured the cultural diversity agenda that was to emerge in the 1990s. These movements were often closely associated with 'alternative' cultural production and distribution circuits comprising experimental theatre groups, rock bands, independent film-makers and cinemas, free radio stations, free festivals, independent recording studios or record labels, small publishing houses, radical bookshops, newspapers and magazines, and visual arts exhibitions or performances in non-traditional venues (Bianchini 2018).

This cultural universe, promoted by those who saw economic opportunity and those concerned with participation, challenged traditional distinctions between 'high' and 'low' cultural forms or classical and popular music. They adopted a very broad definition of 'culture' combining in imaginative ways old and new, highbrow and lowbrow elements. The growing availability of the relatively low-cost new technologies of cultural production used by the new urban social movements increasingly blurred distinctions between commercial and non-commercial, amateur and professional, and consumer and producer (Kelly 1984, 1986). These trends have escalated immensely.

Associated with these movements, then, was the rise of a post-modern aesthetics, both in cultural criticism and artistic production. These questioned traditional notions of cultural value and hierarchy. The new urban social movements influenced many city politicians in Western Europe, mostly of the Left, who expanded the remit of their interventions to include popular and commercial forms of culture. They recognized that cultural policy could act as a vehicle both for mobilizing people in the battle of ideas and for legitimizing their party and to construct forms of city identity which could be shared by people from different neighbourhoods and belonging to different communities of interest. Slowly art-form-based policy moved to a broader-based cultural policy.

Crucial evidence about the social effects of the arts began to emerge in the late 1990s (Matarasso 1997). It became clear that comprehensive redevelopment should not only be physical and focused on economic value creation, but also needs to consider the social impacts on local communities. The pendulum had swung too far. The trickle-down effect which was part of this strategy did not happen. It argues that reducing taxes on businesses and the wealthy stimulates investment and ultimately benefits everyone. Social and community-based arts activism and advocacy gained increasing traction, and cultural funding bodies began to adapt their policies. They looked to widen audiences, and focused more on inclusion or social engagement.

A recent expression of this substantive turnaround that can be tracked in many countries is the British 'Creative People and Places' (CPP) programme launched in 2013, which will have invested more than €50 million by 2020, focusing on community-driven cultural programmes. For instance, 91 per cent of audiences come from neighbourhoods with low or medium levels of arts engagement.[1]

The social fervour we saw in the late 1990s, yet different in form and content, has re-emerged in the 2010s, starting with the Occupy movement in 2011 and continuing in 2018 with School Strike for Climate Change, initiated by Greta Thunberg, and the Extinction Rebellion, coincidentally founded near where I live in Stroud.

The changing repertoire

Needs, priorities and potential assets change, as does the repertoire. Culture-based approaches to development were significant in their time and remain so. They have now become common practice, repeated the world over.

New urgencies have emerged that need to shift the focus of our creativities. Overriding everything today are three concerns:

- Climate-change-related issues from decarbonizing the economy to shifting to cradle to cradle thinking and a circular economy.
- Adjusting to diversity in all its forms, from migration flows in cities and how we can live together in relative harmony to issues of how our identities are shaped in a nomadic world.

1 http://www.creativepeopleplaces.org.uk/our-impact.

- Creating integrated planning and governance systems to address the complexity of the world when our traditions favour siloed approaches.

Over the last decade myriad solutions to address these concerns have been advanced, from innovations to trap carbon and to create 'green coal', to developing biofuels and producing hydrogen-hybrid ships that are emissions-free, and eco-radicalism is now back. On diversity, countless examples of integrating migrants into the workforce or reducing prejudice by involving locals and migrants in collaborative activities such as theatre performances can be seen from more than a hundred members of the 'intercultural cities network' hosted by the Council of Europe. On integrated planning we have a long way to go, and this quest is neither new nor ground-breaking. It is a reiteration of the well-established agenda of synchronizing policy making, as cities need to move from cooperation to coordination to integration. The rhetoric of 'holistic', 'joined-up' or 'integrated' strategy making and service delivery continues, and is increasing in urgency as complex interrelated issues such as homelessness or inequality cannot be addressed without addressing their wider conditions. Bergen is a good example, with its Interagency Cooperation Centre, a cluster of intertwined agencies vital to the city's everyday functioning and crisis management, set up for the Road Cycling World Championships in 2017. The biggest problem was coordinating the 31 agencies in charge of critical services, ranging from private companies to public agencies belonging to the city, region or state. The results were astonishing. Interagency cooperation resolved problems in minutes, that normally would take hours or days. Crucially incidents were solved before they became large and expensive.

Pioneering cities such as Copenhagen, Zurich, Hamburg, Freiburg, Vancouver, Portland and Curitiba are leading the way creatively in green terms, and a new range of awards such as the Green Capital of Europe highlights achievements to encourage copying. Equally the European Diversity Awards seek to build the argument that there is a diversity dividend.

References

Bianchini, Franco (2018), 'Reflections on the origins, interpretations and development of the creative city idea', in Ilja Van Damme, Bert De Munck and Andrew Miles (eds),

Cities and Creativity from the Renaissance to the Present, New York: Routledge, pp. 23–42.

Kelly, Owen (1984), *Community, Art and the State: Storming the Citadels,* Stroud, UK: Comedia.

Kelly, Owen (1986), *Culture and Democracy: The Manifesto,* Stroud, UK: Comedia.

Matarasso, Francois (1997), *Use or Ornament?: The Social Impact of the Arts,* Stroud, UK: Comedia.

11 The gentrification dilemma

Artists and creative professionals as the driver

Gentrification, the process of renewing degraded urban neighbour-hoods, mostly has a negative ring. And that ring has been, for some, associated with the creative city agenda. Displacement is the word that comes to mind, especially of lower-income families and local shops, as well as shifting the racial or ethnic balance of an area. With neighbour-hood improvements, historic rental structures often disappear, and prices rise as more affluent people move in and affordable housing declines, so older residents or businesses cannot afford to stay. It can result in higher local taxes. Most importantly it can lead to a loss of cultural and social diversity and the texture of local civic life. This can lead to community resentment and conflict. It has been a major issue for decades.

Yet there is a flip side. Making places more attractive, gentrification if you like, can improve the quality of life of a neighbourhood and arrest decline, and so stabilize an area by providing more facilities, such as parks and other amenities; it can reduce crime levels, and the rising property values can provide an incentive for owners to improve and upgrade their housing. Gentrification can be positive when the ben-efits, such as a greater feeling of safety, new amenities and a possibly better local economy, outweigh the housing costs. Poorer as well as better-off people equally approve – both like better facilities.

There are progressive approaches to bring out the better side of gentri-fication. When the balance between public and private ownerships and resourcing is good, public interest objectives can be insisted on, and it is possible to bend market forces towards bigger-picture aims, such as providing social housing and maintaining a social mix. Comprehensive renewal that addresses overall well-being and recouples social and eco-nomic agendas as well as fairness is about choice making, and that involves power and politics.

It is easy today for the know-it-all people to claim artists or designers are the shock troops of gentrification, or to claim, as the famous graffiti said, 'artists are the vanguard of gentrification'. The gentrification that was mostly linked to artists when they moved to older, underused or near derelict sites did cities a favour. They either halted decline or gave often edgy, even scary places an uplift, in the process not only making them safer but also generating activities themselves and triggering wider spin-offs. The formula is now well known, but when it started big time in the mid-1980s it saved many areas from steep decline – cafés with a good, grungy style set up initially, focused on their artists community, then restaurants follow, and before you know it the area seems interesting. Unconventional shops set up, as do junk shops and second-hand clothing stores; experimental galleries or performance venues come in, as do unusual hotels, and in the blink of an eye the professionals arrive, especially architects, followed by co-working spaces and incubators units. These third spaces are then flooded with people running around – today especially – with their laptops. Everyone is doing a project or planning one in their portfolio existence, where it takes several jobs to make ends meet. Initially, everyone was attracted by the low prices, and unfortunately it is often precisely those groups who initiated the developments that have had to move out and on to new cheap horizons.

We cannot blame artists per se for triggering this process. What changed was when the more alert property development community noticed this upgrading process and consciously encouraged artists to move into their degraded industrial properties on short-term leases. Then, when the price uplift happened, with notable exceptions, they were forced out. This process was first documented by Sharon Zukin in her book *Loft Living* (1982) describing the New York Manhattan scene from the 1970s onwards. That process continues unabated, so in New York it started at its first hip East Village and then moved on to Hell's Kitchen followed by West Village and then Williamsburg, and now those same hipsters who fled from Manhattan to Brooklyn in the mid-2000s are skipping over to Bushwick, always in search of 'authenticity'.

Green activists as the driver

Rethinking what an asset can be has led to new park ideas, and these improvements in turn regenerate places and inevitably lead to gentrification pressures. Think of the High Line idea, a linear park on a former goods rail line once blighted and abandoned that opened in New York in 2009. It was inspired by the Promenade Plantée in Paris, a 4.7 km tree-lined walkway that is an elevated linear park built on top of an obsolete railway and opened in 1993. The notion of greening is increasingly being copied and adapted, as demonstrated by the Klunkerkranich garden and club in *Neukölln*, Berlin on the top parking deck of a declining and now revitalized shopping centre. Or Transbay Transit Center in San Francisco, an inter-modal transport hub that has an extensive rooftop garden. Another example is the linear park structures across 11th Street Bridge Park in Washington. These are all catalytic symbols.

From High Lines came the idea of Low Lines, as in the Baana in Helsinki which opened in 2012, a rails-to-trails project that converted an old subterranean rail line into a hike and bike trail where you travel through a tree-lined and planted mini ravine. This immediately became the second-busiest non-motorized pathway in the city. It is a Finnish interpretation of New York City's High Line. Another similar project is the Bankside, London project or the proposed Radbahn under the Berlin metro. All are part of the movement to 'Copenhagenize' cities, a concept invented by Mikael Colville-Andersen, a Canadian-Danish urban designer and urban mobility expert (Colville-Andersen 2018). This shifts the urban planning paradigm away from cars to a walking and cycling focus, and implies retrofitting cities dramatically. And it increases urban quality of life and so inevitably lifts values.

It is, thus, not only artists that trigger the gentrification impact. The 'High Line Halo Effect' has a similar logic when public parks in unusual settings either regenerate or uplift an area. The added value to properties overlooking the High Line has been astonishing and estimated at several billion dollars given the increase in tourism, with now seven million visitors to the High Line annually. Already by 2014 an evaluation estimated that New York had received increased tax revenues from the impact of the High Line of about $900 million, and that leaves aside the increase in property values overlooking the line, where you see adverts saying 'Apartments for sale overlooking the High Line'. In an interview with Robert Hammond, one of the initiators, he stated to me: 'My greatest regret was not creating a mechanism to capture value, we still have to struggle to raise funding for the upkeep of the park every year.' *Value capture* is a crucial concept and requires thinking imaginatively about how to develop regulations and incentives to provide a payback to those like eco-activists and artists who improve a city. For instance, a direct and dedicated tax on properties whose value has increased.

Given these overall trends, it explains why creative city making cannot only be about property, but instead must be part of a wider strategy that takes the dynamic context into account. Funding bodies, especially those involved in culture, could have averted the endless process whereby those that initiate regeneration have to move on or find it difficult to finance themselves. For example, arts councils worldwide find it largely impossible to help cultural organizations build their asset base. This could either involve buying the freeholds on behalf of organizations or by acting as a guarantor for a loan. They help refurbishment schemes or with equipment purchases, so borrowing against those assets is not possible. Even though arts councils project themselves as development agencies, in reality they tend to lock funded organizations into a dependency relationship. Not-for-profits, in particular, would benefit from the possibilities and rigorous responsibilities that using assets entail.

The most emblematic example for me, that resulted in a failure, was in 1985 in Birmingham. With Comedia, my organization, we were commissioned by the municipality to look at the light industrial area adjacent to their city centre, called Digbeth. It had obvious potential – it resonated with the history of 'the city of a thousand trades' when it had been a workshop of the world full of small, highly skilled firms producing a huge range of products. The built fabric, mostly solid, often empty, at times dilapidated yet not shoddy enough to be pulled down, was clearly waiting for new purposes. In the mid-1980s the new media industries were beginning to emerge, and we felt it could become a media zone – in essence a creative quarter – where the complete value chain of that sector could be clustered. We knew that the instant you name an area the media zone it sounds cool and of the moment, and by revealing the strategy astute property developers would buy in immediately so prices would rise.

Our idea was simple: to get the council to buy properties that were being offered at throwaway prices and to hold these in a fund as an endowment whose income would support various forms of creative activity and social enterprise – forever – in the future. An investment then of £500,000 would have bought a dozen buildings and solidified the area with an interesting new character. Unfortunately, legally, the municipality was not allowed to do this, although in our view it was one of the wisest ways to spend resources – sums they spent many times over on other things like a one-off festival or upgrading a square, or on a programme of consultancy reports. Being able to use ownership and assets effectively is a central element of sustainability.

References

Colville-Andersen, Mikael (2018), *Copenhagenize: The Definitive Guide to Global Bicycle Urbanism*, Washington, DC: Island Press.
Zukin, Sharon (1982), *Loft Living: Culture and Capital in Urban Change*, Baltimore, MD: Johns Hopkins University Press.

12 Ambition and creativity[1]

Becoming and being more creative or fulfilling a vision does not happen out of nowhere; rather, it is often triggered by a crisis, when people say 'we cannot go on like this', 'we have to rethink'. It requires ambition – a quality often neglected. Cities or people do not suddenly think 'let's be creative'. In some cases there is already a tradition driven by historic circumstances, such as when Venice rose as a Mediterranean power, and its key role as a centre of the emerging printing industry made it a hub of ideas exchange and inventiveness, although in time its creativity declined as its power eroded. It is now a shadow of its former glory, an astonishing place whose lifeblood has been drained by too many tourists. Think of the courageous Basque seafarers reaching out to North America in search of whaling grounds in the 17th century. This required varied inventions in shipbuilding. Think of how Glasgow emerged when leading figures like James Watt improved the steam engine in Glasgow, which generated a new industry. Inspirational people, then, shape the DNA of a city. Here the question is 'does history help push cities forward or does it hold them back?'

It depends, as history is complex. Whether it is a trigger for creativity, learning and innovation is open to question. A historical track record in generating creativity and learning capacity can both constrain or inspire. At times it motivates, at other times it becomes a burden or weight. At its best it generates chains of innovation which rely on the historical precedent of 'master' (*sic*) passing on skills to apprentices, of educational institutions developing reputations and expertise to reinforce a self-sustaining process of confidence, invention and collaboration. At its worst historical success can create arrogance, stasis and resistance to change along the lines of 'We have seen it all before'.

Some say that beautiful as Florence is today it is more a place that merely reflects and reinforces past glories. A danger is that self-

---

1 This chapter draws on Landry (2015).

AMBITION AND CREATIVITY   119

satisfaction and complacency take hold and override the atmosphere. This can generate a sense of closure to outsiders and result in a lack of new ideas.

Industrial Prato nearby, by contrast, without the weight of history and expectation, states that it has 'innovation in the DNA of its textile district' that derives from its wool-processing tradition and continues to evolve with changing market circumstances. This demands that it remains creative to survive in a very competitive context. This in turn has helped develop a thriving arts scene which connects well to its fashion focus.

Consider too another example, namely Bilbao today. Twenty years ago, any European survey of transformation model cities included Bilbao in the top rank alongside others such as Barcelona, Glasgow, Rotterdam or the Emscher Park area in the Ruhr. Interestingly the major capitals Paris or London were then rarely mentioned. Renowned for its creative physical transformation, with the Guggenheim museum the icon, but also including the Santiago Calatrava airport, the Norman Foster metro system and wonderful public space management, Bilbao faces new challenges. Many claim it is in danger of resting on its deserved laurels for creating the 'Bilbao Effect'. This creates an atmosphere where people feel 'we have already achieved and let's not threaten that' and 'don't rattle the boat'. There is a danger that the city will fall into graceful decline. To move forward, another level of ambition is required to keep Bilbao at the forefront in areas like the green economy; interesting, human-centred uses of digitization connected to the creative economy sectors; or having farsighted governance arrangements.

The identity and distinctiveness that history provides becomes an anchor and rooting. It can create a bond between people with different institutional interests cooperating for the common good of the city. However, when identity and distinctiveness degenerate into parochialism, introversion, chauvinism and antagonism to the outside world, they may destroy the foundations of a creative milieu and create a sense of claustrophobia and threat.

Most cities have faced a crisis. Perhaps a traditional industry has declined, or its trading role has been superseded by others. And this is where ambition needs to come in, and where a city says 'It's not OK to be OK'. The archetype presented below derives from a survey of 30

European cities including Lyon, St-Etienne, Mannheim, Manchester, Torino, Oporto, Groningen, Graz and smaller places like Kirklees.[2]

Ambition is a significant word. It is a quality that generates energy, motivation and passion from which other possibilities flow such as being imaginative and more creative. It can jump-start processes of change as key people think *'it is not OK to only be OK'*. It precedes vision and is different and more important. It is the precondition from which a vision might evolve. It helps people concentrate on both the essentials and the bigger picture, and it provides the engine from which commitment grows so that ideas can turn into realities. Ambition needs a purpose and a goal. It is not merely about thrusting to be ahead. The aim is for a place to be successful and to provide the scope for its people, organizations and the city as a whole to be the best they can, given their physical, intellectual and cultural assets. This involves choices about what success means. These choices reflect beliefs and attitudes based on value judgements. It involves using politics as well as exerting power and influence to turn these values into policies and projects on the ground.

An ideal city of ambition has special features, qualities and attributes. They appear here as a simple sequence or model, but reality is never quite like that. Ambitious places recognize that their context and operating *conditions have changed dramatically.* They conclude that a business-as-usual approach will not get them to where they want to be, and understand that the resources and assets that gave them success will not continue to do so in the future. They appreciate that the attitudes and attributes that made them great in the past may hinder them in the future. They know they need to value creativity.

The *best cities start with values* about what is important to them in the longer term. On this basis they establish principles they are truly committed to, that guide their actions. At their most general these might be about providing opportunities for citizens and fostering sustainable development, yet they must not be too obvious. Statements no one would disagree with gain little traction, so, for instance, the wish to be sustainable needs a compelling narrative and actions attached to it.

Practical places assess their situation honestly and *overcome the power of denial.* This in itself involves courage, also a key attribute of creativ-

---

2 https://charleslandry.com/panel/wp-content/themes/twentyeleven/books/Cities-Ambition.pdf.

ity. They understand their position and seek help from the best experts they can find to analyse their condition and prospects. They recognize the nature of the competitive environment around them; they review their resources and how they can be used in the new conditions they have to confront.

They tackle the really difficult problems head-on and *engage with criticism*, and they can be seen to be working just where the problem is. They are willing to be unpopular. Ambitious places use crisis as means to reassess potential, and this can help transform problems into opportunities. They are willing to pay a price for things that might not work and accept the costs. They know you cannot win it all.

They involve the people, organizations and sectors in their city and *listen to their constituencies*, and especially *trust their youth* and go with their enthusiasms. This opens out possibilities, and that process could be called creative.

The bigger-picture view they paint is open, so everyone can find a place in it and people can be involved as co-creators. This fosters widespread ownership and commitment. Such a grand picture, a better word than vision, is broad enough to inspire, but narrow enough to enable practical tasks to happen. This develops a mood of success and involvement which is encouraged not as a matter of charity, but as belief in the collective power of sharing responsibility.

Leaders explain the direction of travel, but with flexibility in the plan so that space is opened for dialogue. They are ready to accept other ideas as plans evolve. This fosters a shared sense of identity to allow different voices to thrive. They do not subscribe to the heroic version of urban reinvention, and they *build a team and set of networks* around themselves. This establishes a widespread leadership grouping. Together they discuss and identify catalysts and game changers. However, at the beginning, a charismatic person or group – perhaps a mayor or a partnership – can set the transformation process in motion. The subsequent task is to embed the change culture within the leadership groupings that follow. This allows the many to find their creativity potential.

This provides the confidence to *challenge the accepted canon*, a precondition of creativity, and overcome the inevitable inertia in many spheres – perhaps the method of operation of the governance structure, bureaucracy or cultural institutions, or perhaps the fact that vested economic interests might only go for the tried and tested. An open and flexible approach is adopted that dares to risk uncertainty or failure, as good leaders as well as others know that without experimenting and testing out ideas and projects, bigger gains or successes will be more difficult to achieve. They create conditions where *people and organizations can be imaginative* and look for possibilities and hidden resources laterally. The atmosphere created means that challenges are seen as opportunities in disguise.

Along the way, by learning from doing, they *rethink the processes and procedures* and so gently persuade, using good examples to overcome organizational rigidities. They realize that getting things done involves partnering, so all sectors have to rethink how they operate and what their distinctive contribution can be. The *public administration becomes less controlling* and more enabling, and the private sector understands that fostering the public interest helps them in the longer term so their business-driven energy can combine both profit and public good. Good places find room for community or activist groups and critics to bring ideas and solutions to the joint city-making endeavour.

To become effective and to show achievements that create confidence, the best cities *think big and start small*, as being incremental allows flexibility to be built in.

Confident creative cities go with the *grain of their local culture*; they start with themselves and build from that. They learn from good appropriate examples from elsewhere but do not imitate mindlessly. They adapt good practice to their special conditions and thus act out their uniqueness. To distinguish between fads and fashion and deep trends is understood as important, as being trendy can often push a place in a false direction.

Identifying clear new roles and purposes for a city is a major step, and strategies and action plans need to be aligned with them. Freiburg's focus on becoming a paragon of the green city is one example, Malmo becoming a university city centred on cross-disciplinary courses is another, and Eindhoven rethinking its industrial base driven by sophisticated partnerships is a third. Their success is based on understanding resources.

Building a *strong evidence base* to create legitimacy is a vital ingredient in the process of change. Then outlining a step-by-step action programme incorporating staging posts and early winners, starting with easier, cheaper, shorter-term initiatives, helps prepare for difficult, more expensive longer-term projects. Manchester's re-emergence has used this approach. This trajectory anchors a paced and purposeful approach that helps gain credibility. This allows time for reflection even though many want to rush. It also requires adopting new measurements for success and failure.

Leading players possess and express passion at times, and they show their love for their city, even emotionally. This keeps up energy and motivation, and for them their city is a vocation. They are driven because they want to make things happen and so build momentum to both generate energy and unleash and harness potential. These actors try 'to be in it rather than above it', so become directly involved.

Narrating a story that builds emotion plays a part, as does using the past as a basis for moving into the future. This grows confidence and can help turn negatives around. To be willing to use unorthodox methods for getting issues across or to solve problems is crucial, as doing the ordinary well only goes so far. The best go further; they risk and experiment.

These ambitious creative places try to *communicate well with a real simplicity* of message and clarity of purpose, and they work with symbols and emblematic initiatives, *having identified meaningful catalysts*. This way they are more likely to get buy-in, by telling the story in the right way. It also gets the many to own the transformation. In this overall approach, they facilitate, stimulate, regulate and enthuse. This means working the connections and networks heavily. Instead of exerting power they trade it for enhanced creative influence. They set aside vanity for the many to take part in the glory. The capacity to self-regenerate emerges from this.

All this is only possible if there is strong partnership capacity, so ambitious places instigate quadruple helix linkages between the public and private sectors, the universities and wider communities of interest. This helps convince governments to assist.

Orchestration is the watchword as good city making is complex and needs to bring the disparate elements together; harvesting the benefits of this broad rethinking takes time, a long time.

The primary conclusions are that the creative capacity of a place is shaped by its history, its culture, its physical setting and its overall operating conditions. This determines its character and 'mindset'.

Reference

Landry, Charles (2015), *Cities of Ambition*, Stroud, UK: Comedia.

13 Psychology and the city[1]

'What is the city but the people.'
Shakespeare's *Coriolanus*

'*We shape* our buildings; thereafter they *shape* us.'
Winston Churchill

'It is ironic that we know more about the habitat of mountain gorillas than
we do about the habitat of people.'
Jan Gehl

To understand the broader scope within which people experience
where and who they are we need to explore an emerging, largely hidden
dimension in creative city making. This is the link between the personality of a city and those of the individuals within it – an idea I have
explored with my colleague Chris Murray. To be creative requires not
only certain personality traits, but also an urban context – a milieu –
that helps reinforce it. Psychological dimensions determine our capacity to address the big issues that really matter, from climate change,
to addressing inequality, to achieving economic growth (Garretsen et
al. 2019). Being in a city is a two-way psychological process. The city
impacts upon our mind and our mental and emotional state impacts
upon the city. This is part of a constant cycle of influencing and being
influenced, perpetual transactions changing moment to moment as our
daily lived experience unfolds, with repercussions both for us and for the
city in ways we cannot always be aware of. Revealing these interactions
and their impacts is important in understanding how we can make,
manage and inhabit places, how we make the best of opportunities or
deal with entrenched problems. It creates a focus on our well-being.

To see the urban fabric, its forms, its dynamics and city life as
empty shells devoid of human psychological content or its life story

---

1 This chapter draws on Landry and Murray (2017).

is careless. To be blind to its consequences is foolish, because in a significant sense *the city is primarily an emotional experience with psychological effects.*

It is astonishing then that psychology, the area of study that explores the dynamics of feeling and emotion, has not been taken sufficiently seriously as an urban discipline, not only by psychology itself but also by urban decision makers, since it seeks to understand why we act the way we do. Crucially the personal psychological dispositions and mindsets of those who shape cities also determine our urban life, hopefully to improve our overall well-being and resilience, for us to mature and to deal with adversity and live fulfilling lives. Psychology concerns itself with individuals, organizations and groups, but, with notable exceptions, not the city.

The city is not a lifeless thing. *People have personality and identity, and, as they are congregations of people, so do cities.* The 'urban psyche' could be described as the complex personality that emerges from the interactions between people and place. Urban psychology is the evolving science of understanding more about this urban psyche, alongside our own psychological response to cities, and is about how we can use that knowledge to affect how cities are shaped.

The city powerfully affects our motivations, habits and behaviour, which in turn determine the success or failure of our projects and programmes, of our city making in general, and also how a city feels. Consider simply how ugly places generate a sense of hopelessness and lack of care, or how ones seen as more beautiful or interesting, although we can argue about what that is, can lift energies. Understanding the psychology of places and how their history and life shapes what they are is a vital missing thread in urban thinking and will help us create better cities more in tune with our deeper feelings and needs.

The focus on cities and their psychology is the latest step in an evolving long-term endeavour to reshape and enrich city making and to shift its intellectual architecture. This started 30 years ago, by connecting creativity, culture and the city together as the driving forces in cities' adaptation to change and reinvention. The culture of a place, its origins, its history, its location, its resources is etched into and shapes how a city acts, determining its prospects. How creative a place can be is determined partly by its culture, and its culture is determined by its psychological make-up.

The *emphasis on the city not being just a machine but more a living organism* that exists within a sensory landscape highlights the rich register of emotions that are triggered by how it looks and feels. We therefore challenged cities to assess and plan themselves simultaneously through a 'hardware and software' lens, giving equal weighting to measurements concerned with people's lived experience of place and not only those concerned with hard infrastructure or economics. This step brought together the cultural sectors and social sciences.

Seeing the city through a psychological lens is the next step, and an urgent one, as the complexity of issues affecting cities is accelerating, threatening to overwhelm our current policy toolkit. The world is now predominantly urban, with cities growing at a breathtaking pace as 1.5 million people each week move to cities (roughly 200 000+ a day or 140 every minute).

The threats to urban stability are known, especially poverty and inequality. Concerns over economic inequality were shown in one global survey to 'trump all other dangers',[2] and are now an influence in the rise of anti-establishment, populist and nationalist movements, which can in turn play on deep-seated psychological fears.

Our financial means limit the resources available to deal with these issues which can impact on individual and urban security. But this is not just an issue of finance, nor one that can be solved only by more resource. It also requires an understanding of the psychological dynamics that are at play for individuals and groups, and this can lead us towards new solutions that focus the available resources in the most effective way possible. All of these conditions shape how people in a city might be creative, and the urban psychology perspective could in this way have a profound impact.

A growing population exerts pressure on everything, and the mass movement of people across the globe can impact on urban identities explosively if not properly managed. The effects of this density of people can burst out in unexpected and explosive ways. Our inability to grasp these risks and how to deal with them can create intense governance, management but also psychological problems. Dealing with this well requires imagination, practice, feedback loops and continuous learning.

---

2 The survey was a Pew Global Research Project and is quoted in Atkinson (2015).

Internationally concerns are rising over mental health, especially in cities where the percentage of people experiencing these issues is far higher. The reasons are complex and often linked to poverty, but also to living in crowded, noisy, smelly and soulless environments. There is evidence too that the bigger the city, the greater the likely mental health impacts (Adli 2017), and also the greater the awareness of its socio-economic impacts. Psychological skills are themselves often creative, and if they can solve some urban problems like mental health then they are contributing to creating the conditions for people to work at a better level.

Overlaid on this are the delights and discontents of digitization. The ability to be constantly connected, to be 'here and there' simultaneously, as well as the blending of 'real' and virtual worlds, can break focus and fragment our attention. *In a more nomadic world the sense of belonging linked to place can disperse* across networks and geographical boundaries. It can change our conception of space, place and time, affecting how we relate to the city. Add to this the new disruptive technologies such as artificial intelligence or sensing systems and the world feels as if it is on a rollercoaster.

Cities are places where most of us are strangers. They are a mix of people with intensely personal histories, with differing cultures and perspectives, views of life and interests, who have come together to share a collective space. But cities are also the spatial-level par excellence for uniting diverse identities into a common whole, places where face-to-face interaction still really matters as a means of binding and bonding people, building a sense of shared community, citizenship, and stewardship of place.

Revealing and then working with the composite character or psychology of a city can be a powerful tool in understanding what pushes a place forwards or holds it back, what curtails or contributes to its civic life or creative potential, what creates the spirit of a place and how that embeds itself into attitudes and organizational cultures, determining its future.

The hidden dimension

Urban psychology is a way of making visible the hidden patterns and unseen drivers shaping cities. By putting psychology onto the urban agenda this reinforces and affirms *the significance of subjective experience*. It is the combination of quantitative measures, such as location, economic assets or history, and our personal qualitative responses that shape what cities as collective entities are able to do and their achievements. Few would argue that understanding human behaviour is not crucial, or that psychology is not an important discipline.

It is endlessly noted that we live in an urban age, and attempts to understand our evolution to 'homo urbanis', a predominantly urban species, are underway across many disciplines: sociology, anthropology, ethnography, geography, politics, environmental science, economics, design and culture. Researchers have previously looked at the built environment, energy consumption and pollution, food supply and security, health in cities from obesity to depression, movement and mobility, demographics and ageing, and urban agglomeration economics.

This research provides a *growing awareness of the fragility of cities*, the risk nexus of escalating vulnerabilities and stresses in a world of remorseless change. Interconnected global challenges are growing in scale and scope in a way that affects people and cities directly and demands behaviour change.

How can you understand behaviour change or global transitions without understanding psychology? Unfolding events in cities that at first sight may seem illogical can be unscrambled and interpreted by looking at the range of psychological responses people display.

What comes first – history? Culture? Or is it landscape, location or resources that determine a city's destiny? Is it the chicken or the egg? There are complex relationships between these factors, and most have been credited with strong explanatory value. All these circumstances etch themselves into the urban psyche, influencing the culture of place.

Examples and impact

Some cities we call sober, others constrained, thwarted, stifling and reduced or edgy, 'can do' and open or welcoming, among many other adjectives. These *can be described as personality traits both in humans and cities*. Our responses to geography, location, resources and weather can all shape this sense of personality. Contrast the demeanour, attitudes and behaviours of someone from a colder, northern city with those of a person living on the equator, or consider the difference between a person living in a port city and someone living in a city located inland, in mountains or on the plains. Think of people living in a capital city or a satellite. Citizens of different places are perceived as arrogant, vibrant, self-important or subdued. Physical environments too have differing effects. Places perceived as ugly and with endless swathes of asphalt and the ever-present noise and smell of cars can drain the spirit. This can enclose people and make them anxious and uncommunicative. How can they then be inventive – if at a minimum it is curtailed? At the other extreme, places seen as beautiful can lift the senses and engender a feeling that the world is in order or stable and so strengthen confidence and open people up. This yearning for whole-ness is powerful. Can these factors curtail city ambition and prospects? Urban atmospheres differ sharply, as does a sense of confidence, and we need to ask 'what is its deeper source?'

We have a good understanding of how places work in some respects, for example socially, economically or via the ramifications of urban design. But we are far less experienced at tapping into the deeper layers of urban life that may reveal hidden dynamics that can have a causal relationship to success or failure. Without this knowledge, we often interpret outcomes as unexpected or as unintended consequences. Having measured some of these dynamics by looking at the creative capacity of cities over many years,[3] this has revealed hidden attributes that drive a city and determine its future, and these principally have psychological roots. This should not surprise us since cities are their people, the networks, the tribal allegiances and institutions they form. Our conclusion, for instance, in assessing the potential of Mannheim in Germany was that its lack of confidence was the primary issue to be addressed. There is no department for this, and strategies to deal with it involve many activities from nitty-gritty projects to enhance the public environment to celebratory activities.

All these attributes have an impact on how the story of a city unfolds, how it makes the most of its resources and potentials, how it addresses setbacks and dramatic events and how it acts itself out in the world. The collective behaviour of the psyches of individuals and organiza-

---

3 http://charleslandry.com/panel/wp-content/themes/twentyeleven/books/The-Creative-City-Index.pdf.

tions when amalgamated and merged determine the spirit of the city, its atmosphere, its sense of soul.

Ghent, for instance, has a deep-seated attitude of self-criticism. This spurs the city to do better through its continual questioning, even though it can come across as lacking in confidence. The fiercely independent city was often occupied by foreign troops, so history played its part in its psychological response to circumstance.

A cliché about Adelaide in South Australia with a strong element of truth is that the city is intellectual and 'good at talking, less good at walking the walk'. This is not surprising since it was the only city in Australia created by idealistic free-settlers. That progressive foundation enabled it to create positive change, for example by being the first place to give women the full vote in 1894. It can be seen as a little high-minded, with a self-perception that Adelaide is better than all those other upstart cities that have sacrificed a good quality of life in order to chase gaudy ambitions.

Bilbao grapples with forceful natural elements, has a strong exploratory instinct, and has a unique ethno-linguistic background. It was genetically isolated and has the highest proportion of the RH blood group in the world, yet was very influential in sailing exploration, its sailors reaching the icy shores of Northern Canada in the early 1500s, and the Basque explorer Elcano taking over the captaincy of Magellan's ship when he was killed, to complete the first circumnavigation of the world. Castilian dominance has acted to torture its past and affect present ambitions for independence. This has reinforced the sense of pride in Basque identity, and perhaps the city is too proud to be reflective.

Take New Yorkers, how they think of themselves and how others think of them. The city's pressure cooker quality, in which it constantly needs to perform, generates ideas, projects and trade that etches itself into the psyche of the people as a 'can do' place, for better or worse. Big city people walk and eat faster, perhaps think faster – they say 10 per cent more than townspeople. The media images of New York construct and reinforce these perceptions.

London has that odd mix of tradition, creativity and eccentricity where having ideas is easier than making them happen. It is a city whose history and language create a vortex effect drawing in talent from everywhere. Perhaps this can make a city rest on its laurels.

Sydney is a place whose atmosphere is brash, determined and achievement driven whereas, so the cliché goes, Melbourne seeks achievement at a more considered pace and is seen as more refined.

Trieste, feeling it is always stuck at the edge, was obstructed endlessly by Venetian sea power and then later embraced protection from the Habsburgs, whose glittering seaport it became. After World War I a victorious Italy moved into Trieste. The Slovene names were switched to Italian and then followed ongoing border disputes, forced Italianization, Nazi occupation, the decimation of the Jewish population and the formation of the only concentration camp on Italian soil. Today Trieste feels a little sad, like it is looking for a role and a less disturbed identity so it can face the future with clarity.

Mannheim, again, whose string of discoveries include Carl Benz's car, is seen as industrial and ugly, the core of the city being destroyed in World War II, and this external battering leads many Mannheimers to apologize too much. This shapes its self-image and can turn the city inwards. But in its undergrowth, it has one of the most vibrant German music scenes.

We think of Athens with the weight of its gloried past to which the present can never measure up, Beijing with its sense of being at the centre of the world, Tel Aviv as the first all-Jewish city in modern times which maintains its pioneering spirit and is now a global start-up hub, while Dubai's recent explosion onto the world stage is sharply shaping Dubaians' sense of self and destiny.

These city stories and their historic facts can have deep psychological effects, with the past reflected in the present, determining the future for a city as it can do for a person. They are therefore worthy of consideration.

Our 'City Personality Test' can be found at http://urbanpsyche.org/, and readers are asked to explore it and to provide us with feedback under the heading 'My City'.

References

Adli, Mazda (2017), *Stress and the City: Why Cities Make Us Ill. And Why They Are Still Good for Us*, Munich: C. Bertelsmann.

Atkinson, Anthony B. (2015), *Inequality: What Can Be Done?*, Cambridge, MA: Harvard University Press.

Garretsen, Harry I. Janka, Dimitrios Stoker, Ron Martin Soudis and Jason Renfrow (2019), 'The relevance of personality traits for urban economic growth: Making space for psychological factors', *Journal of Economic Geography*, **19** (3), 541–65.

Landry, Charles and Chris Murray (2017), *Psychology and the City: The Hidden Dimension*, Stroud, UK: Comedia.

14 Digitization – the game changer

In what seems like a blink of an eye historically, the digital world has come upon us. It completely transforms what we think being creative is, its scope and reach, and what we imagine a creative city to be. The impact and influence of the digitized city represents a game changer. All-pervasive digitization driven by big data means now that our culture is digital and the digital shapes our culture. It fashions everything in a dramatically changed context. With gathering force from its beginnings, it is now omnipresent. It is like the air we breathe and the electricity that flows. It shifts people's understanding of time, space and place. To make this world happen involved incredible imagination and a vast number of inventions. The question as always is who controls the technology.

Digitization enables us to think of the city and how to use it in different ways, and here the catchword 'third places' is key as these places become increasingly important to the many who can operate from anywhere like nomads.

Digitization represents *a tectonic shift* whose devices, with their disruptive potential, are changing cities, society and social life, connectivity, the economy, cultural life and cultural institutions. Its impacts and influence will be as powerful as the climactic changes that swept through our world with the Industrial Revolution two hundred years ago. Giant turbines and whirring machines symbolized that revolution, whereas this one is more invisible, driven by algorithms etched into small screens. This engenders fear of a world racing uncontrollably ahead, but spawns excitement about the opportunities unfolding. Those who make decisions, the digital settlers, have mostly migrated into this world, whereas for the young, digital natives, it is all they know. This highlights a misalignment, as for the first time in history the young are teaching the old rather than the reverse.

Every new means of production changes the physical and mental landscape and how our systems operate. Its drama is clear when the world's largest taxi company, Uber, owns no taxis; when Facebook, the world's most popular media owner, creates no content; when Alibaba, the most valuable retailer, has no inventory; and when Airbnb is in effect the world's largest hotel chain, but owns no hotels.

Digitization and its power to connect, communicate and manipulate data creates our data-drenched world, driving transformation on a scale that changes the foundations of business and public service affecting every facet of our lives. This data-mining revolution is an innovation accelerator, a Gutenberg 3.0, transforming how we work, manage and organize, what we do, how we create, and how we think. Digitally driven tools and technologies shape the cultures we produce and consume, and how we experience the world.

The digital rides on its third platform, a combination of cloud computing, mobile devices, social media and big data technologies all working together. Here mobile devices and apps extend capabilities, the cloud acts as an outsourced mechanism, big data enables ultra-fast analysis to interpret data and gain insights, and social technologies bring interactive human dimensions into digital, automated processes. Mashing these disparate technologies breaks silos and is turbocharging digital commerce, information analytics and the development of intelligent infrastructures. Google, Amazon, Facebook, Uber, Airbnb and Twitter all use these powerfully. These digital winners and the myriad of start-ups make disruption the norm. The scope, scale, pervasiveness, ubiquity and speed that evolving technologies enable astonishes. Two-and-a-half billion Internet users interact with this system at its simplest by texting messages, and with more complexity by managing household electronic devices from a distance.

Connectivity and data are the new forms of capital, supplanting material resources, finance or location, with the three big game changers being big data, the Internet of Things and intelligent objects.

The cultural landscape on rare occasions is sucked in by the gravitational pull of dynamic technologies and the ideas and tendencies they engender – digitization is one. It is the dominant cultural force of the 21st century, slowly, but firmly, twisting everything into its orbit, engendering a mental and social transformation created by our new electronic environment that blends and mixes the 'virtual' and 'real'. Simulated products, services and augmented reality experiences are extending everywhere, even creating virtual social networks, relationships and feelings.

Here *technology is like oxygen* and increasingly easy to use. Unavoidably we are pulled into its thrall with its fluid, malleable, remixed content, where we graze (the digital form we once called browsing) and dive deep with its permeable boundaries seamlessly sliding into endlessness. The watchwords are open, flexible, interactive, co-creative, agile, connective, instant, immersive, ubiquitous, enabling, sharing, integrative, multitasking, simulated, virtual, fragmenting and constantly online.

In short, we are *in the midst of redesigning the world and all its systems* – legal, moral and political as well as the economy and our infrastructures – for a digital age, with information and communications technology (ICT) as one backbone. This is an immense cultural project. Yet our built environment has been designed for how we lived and worked 50 years ago and more. This fostered functional zoning with living spaces, offices and dirty industry in tidy separation with hubs and spokes piecing the city parts together with roads and metros systems and a city centre with key functions, government offices, the main retail and dominant cultural institutions.

A reverse engineering process is necessary to adapt to the digital age and to create new intelligent infrastructures, sensing technologies and objects that live within its hard-engineered fabric. Sensors help cities respond in smart ways from the simple to the complex. The 'sharing economy' becomes possible, built around sharing human and physical resources. Innumerable apps foster swapping, exchanging or joint purchasing, with car-sharing technology like Zipcars a prime example. Opening data creates easier feedback loops between citizens and city decision makers, so potentially helping to reinvigorate local democracy and making collaborative governance models possible. Indeed, we can say 'the city is software' as its operations are completely software driven.

The 'open source' movement has accelerated the digital world, well-etched into the ethos of free sharing of software between academics during the origins of computing and the Internet. This has enabled collaborative activities between disciplines, so breaking silos, as demonstrated by a rapprochement between the two great ways of exploring, understanding and knowing: science and art. All this can unleash potentials, new ideas and new forms of combinatory creativity.

The volume, velocity and variety of instantly available data streams combined with the *'anytime, anyplace, anywhere' phenomenon* change how we interact with and in space, place and time. Yet place matters as never before despite increased virtual interactions, as people need physical place to anchor themselves. The public realm rises dramatically in importance, and as working patterns change, gathering places and especially third spaces have renewed relevance. This sensorized city largely looks the same but operates and performs differently. Think of how Airbnb, Zipcar, Uber, Lyft or Bridj have reconceived hospitality or urban mobility. All of these developments require inventiveness.

Cities have created spatial experiment zones as laboratories and test beds to force feed new experiments. Cities need safe places to explore given the escalating speed of digitally driven innovations. The Living Labs movement, with now 170 active members worldwide,[1] has a citizen-driven innovation philosophy fitting the co-creative ethos in seeking to turn ideas into real-life contexts. An interesting one is the City of Things project in Antwerp, which embraces the whole city.

The redesign of cities needs bigger values placing humans centre stage and a linked urban culture to anchor its actions. A human perspective should drive technologies rather than the reverse. Technology fever and innovative apps make one forget that technology enables and is a servant of our bigger aims, such as encouraging more empowered citizens. Crucially the innovative impulses unleashed should solve old problems with new economy possibilities, such as addressing inequality or creating quality jobs.

Decision makers have *a once in a lifetime opportunity to rebuild our cities* differently, in a creative way, including harnessing social media capabilities, interactive platforms or open data to deepen democracy so making it more responsive to people's desires and needs. The crucial question is 'will the public interest be put centre stage?' Unfortunately that remains constantly under threat. Cities must remain alert to ensure that their priorities and values are acknowledged, as the digital industrial complex has discovered the city as a major new market. Crucially we should not only talk about new hardware infrastructures but instead also of empowering people to be 'smart citizens'.

---

1 http://www.openlivinglabs.eu/aboutus.

Undeniably, untold promises and opportunities to improve our quality of life are possible by making life more citizen centric, more local, more convenient or efficient and seamlessly connected. These positives mesh, as with all new technologies, with dangers. They are both liberating and potentially invasive and dangerous, as with the rise of fake news. The most pressing dangers are control by algorithms or the watchful eye of surveillance, suffering overload from constant data cascading over us or unemployment created by intelligent robots. Merging computing power and vast archives of data enables robots to perform all predictable jobs and increasingly hollows out middle-income employment.

The communications revolution has broken the public sector data monopoly as everyone has access to knowledge on their devices. The digital unleashes abilities to mobilize opinion and movements, of which the Arab Spring, the Occupy movement, the Five Star Movement in Italy and Podemos in Spain are examples. Tactical urbanism projects (Lydon and Garcia 2015), such as 'parking day', 'restaurant day', 'better block' or 'guerrilla gardening', stem from the same ethos. Social media savvy, they enable citizens to unite while not meeting physically. They change how the city and citizens communicate and make decisions – this is radical civics in action.[2] This harnesses community intelligence, whereas historically community responsibilities were outsourced to public administrations, which were service production engines. This implies a culture shift, with transparency permeating the culture.

To keep the best of this innovation dynamic requires policy priorities within a governance and incentives framework that harmonizes fairness, transparency, public access and the right to privacy. This balancing act must navigate between sanctioning, enabling and supporting, and containing, curtailing and controlling. It includes a MyData agenda to safeguard privacy and allow people to manage their own data; to be continually alert to balance public and private benefits; to foster a new civic culture that is determined to be co-creative; to create rules and codes for the sensorized city, the city of interactive surfaces and immersive digital environments;[3] creating a mixed-partnership 'thinking brain' with an agile organizational form that learns to understand weak signals on the horizon. Digital literacy is crucial for understanding what is going on; for instance, algorithms

---

2 https://www.opendemocracy.net/ash-amin/reinventing-democracy.
3 https://eu-smartcities.eu/content/urban-platforms.

help us to move from 'descriptive to predictive and prescriptive analytics' and doing data analysis in real time.[4] Where is autonomous judgement in this scenario?

The urban experience

There is a seductive quality to this digitized city. It sucks you softly into its interactive web where with a swipe and a click you can be gratified – mostly instantly. Here is ubiquitous Wi-Fi; here we move easily between the worlds of 'here and there', that is, local, global, physically real and virtual. Mobile devices provide mobility so we can work on the fly, be up to date and where our vast library, the Internet, provides untold knowledge resources. Every social group is participating, yet those operating fully 'on the move' remain the minority. But it is not only high-level professionals or digital nomads: bus and lorry drivers, nurses, shop staff, dentists, museum attendants or construction workers equally have digital resources and increasingly operate on the hoof.

This city communicates through every fibre of its being. It is dynamic: signs move, billboards tell stories, info boards inform. It has a filmic quality; you sense you are floating. Yet the buildings still have solidity. Serendipity is consciously orchestrated as meeting places and third places grow from park benches to the café. This changes our work environment, with portfolio working becoming more dominant. Classic offices in rapid decline feel constrained and were down in number by 33 per cent in 2015 since their peak in 2009.

The digitized cityscape enables global brands to dominate our sensescape and visual experience. This has emotional and psychological effects on urban dwellers given the dangers of sense overload and overstimulation. Some cities like São Paolo, Paris and Tokyo are now seeking to control this proliferation in the public interest.

Increasingly artists are used to create the installation events that generate this urban experience. We see buildings transform, occasionally with sudden subversive, temporary elements to keep our attention. Louis Vuitton is a master, with its link with Yayoi Kusama the most famous. Vuitton's 2012 collection was inspired by her polka dots and seen in 460 stores in 64 countries.

---

4 http://idcdocserv.com/1678.

This urban branding process has special power at night. Public entities struggle to compete in projecting useful information from transport timetables, pollution monitoring, weather conditions, events or alerts.

The *'smart city'* notion has challenged the creative city idea, although it is very different given its technology focus. It has a powerful rhetoric and involves using information and communication capacities to increase performance and reduce resource use. It was initially promoted by big tech companies who identified the city as a major market and bulk purchaser of products and services to make life more convenient, efficient, secure, self-regulating and predictable. Companies were criticized as they did not initially focus on citizen engagement.[5] This apparently free-for-all digital landscape is largely patrolled by what Dan Hill calls the 'Urban Intelligence Industrial Complex' led by IBM, Cisco, General Electric, Siemens, Philips and search engines like Google or Yahoo.[6]

The 'smart' word is slippery and in danger of overuse. It now means making the most of a city's human, technical and ecological resources to increase the quality of life, 'doing more with less' or being clever in using ICT. The inherent promise of digitization and Global Positioning System (GPS) technology is that we can re-create social bonds and interactions more locally. Eurocities summarizes well the perspective from a public interest view: 'Becoming a smarter city is not an end goal, but a continuous process to be more resource efficient whilst simultaneously improving quality of life.'[7]

There is no one-size-fits-all: becoming smarter means different things to different cities; but there can be no smart city without smart citizens.

> Smarter cities should be inclusive places that use technology and innovation to empower, engage with and capitalise on citizen participation. Engaging citizens goes beyond the uptake of technology: it extends to co-creating ideas and solutions by encouraging new governance and transparency tools such as living labs, integrating citizen input in urban planning with spaces and support for start-ups. Successful smart cities facilitate this

5 http://www.theguardian.com/cities/2014/dec/17/truth-smart-city-destroy-democracy-urban-thinkers-buzzphrase.

6 http://www.thescavenger.net/media-a-technology-sp-9915/61-mediatech2/73-postmodernism-is-out-digimodernism-is-in.html.

7 Interview with Nikolaos Kontinakis, senior policy coordinator, Eurocities.

participation, co-creation and co-production with citizens and other local partners.[8]

Eindhoven's intelligent lighting strategy, for instance, creates responsive streets, even helping dementia patients to find their way. Amsterdam's 'Social sensing on demand', now being replicated in other places, allows citizens to provide feedback on any emerging condition, from potential flooding to broken pavements. The 'smart bins' projects in Barcelona and elsewhere help bin lorries only pick full bins to empty, as sensors communicate to drivers.

The social and the shared

Every medium of communication changes the city and how we interact with it. Each transformation has increased social possibilities – sociability grew with the ability to catch a train, to drive a car, to make a phone call. It has not declined with the Internet, and social media escalates possibilities. The issue is the quality of interaction. Does our online social life, catalysed by permanent connectivity, complement our offline world by enriching our overall life experience, or does it replace it, leading to some loss? Communication in the flesh gives us the physical and emotional. Crucially sociability increases the scope for being creative through its increased exchange of ideas, being challenged or finding partners.

The desire for and necessity of community has not changed, but how it is expressed has – less bound in the fixed physical spaces of a traditional community limited to family and a few outsiders. Our more nomadic life allows us to affiliate and identify ourselves in multiple ways, defined more by, and embedded in, our networks than classic bonds. Networks define community in a nomadic world. Its flip side are the negative networks where undesirables can find each other more easily.

Place matters in our shifting landscape. It provides anchorage, belonging, opportunity, connection and, ideally, inspiration. Here, online and offline, cyberspace and local space combine to make identity, shape interests and generate a meaningful life. This manifests itself in how

---

8 http://www.eurocities.eu/eurocities/documents/EUROCITIES-statement-on-smart-cities-WSPO-9WQDQ9.

cities work, are designed and navigated. The public realm, from pavements to benches, pocket parks and well-designed covered areas rise dramatically in importance, as do third places, like informal cafés (Oldenburg 1999). These are essential for community building – communal yet homely but always with free Wi-Fi. Greater connectivity and faster Internet have liberated people to work from home as telecommuters or on the move. Third places are key as welcoming, accessible spaces. There is power in being alone together. The collective urban experience will take on added importance in future. This all reminds us of the creative quarters that developed from the 1990s onwards, but more turbocharged. With fragmented communication channels the norm, this is why a festivals culture and spectacular events, artistically driven, frame an increasingly significant part of urban culture. Third places exist too in the virtual realm with online communities, whose qualities mirror those of physical communities and where relative freedom from social status is a boon.

Our bias to be social[9,10] provides a genetic basis to the addictive qualities of increasingly visually driven social media. The world is dramatically transforming from the dominance of word- and text-based communication to the visual, with scientists highlighting the 'picture superiority effect'.[11] Advances in pattern recognition software linked to artificial intelligence and self-learning systems make manipulating the visual easier. This explains the rise in image-based social media platforms. Add to this the power of infographics – a merger of visuals and text. The advertising industry draws on this in a continual drive to grab attention, so changing the city landscape.

The Internet engages us in untold worlds; it changes the way the mind works, but can encroach and invade, creating cognitive overload which breaks concentration, fragments attention and disconnects us from life. Staying centred in a tech-saturated world is not easy. No wonder 'mindfulness' is all the rage. Perhaps the future of creativity in this world will be enhanced by shutting off and detoxing digitally.

---

9 http://kreativproces.dk/http:/kreativproces.dk/wp-content/uploads/2010/08/Dunbars-tal-og-reseach.pdf.

10 https://blog.bufferapp.com/psychology-of-social-media.

11 https://www.researchgate.net/profile/Terry_Childers/publication/239278291_Conditions_for_a_Picture-Superiority_Effect_on_Consumer_Memory/links/00b7d529ce9df9422a000000.pdf.

References

Landry, Charles, (2016), *The Digitized City: Influence & Impact*, Stroud, UK, Comedia.

Lydon, Mike and Anthony Garcia (2015), *Tactical Urbanism: Short-Term Action for Long-Term Change*, Washington, DC: Island Press.

Oldenburg, Ray (1999), *The Great Good Place: Cafés, Coffee Shops, Bookstores, Bars, Hair Salons, and Other Hangouts at the Heart of a Community*, New York: Marlowe and Company.

15 The creative bureaucracy

Berlin, September 2018, and 1300 people are gathered for the Creative Bureaucracy Festival, where speakers from 20 countries in 170 sessions are exploring how we can rethink and revalue public administration. Subsequently, in 2019, a number of cities across Europe hold similar events in Amsterdam, Bergen, Birmingham, Lisbon, Valencia and Vienna, with a second festival in Berlin.[1] Why has this suddenly happened? Is this a movement in the making? Perhaps this is the final missing element in the creative city agenda.

They are showing the many new ways of running the public sector and that bureaucracies are not necessarily stuffy if given half a chance. Many examples are summarized too in *The Creative Bureaucracy and Its Radical Common Sense*, a book that I co-wrote with Margie Caust (Landry and Caust 2017).

The answer to the 'why' is that public bureaucracies globally face a converging, escalating crisis. Our societies are increasingly unequal. The population is ageing. There are fewer resources to respond to growing needs for care services. Demands for affordable living conditions are increasing. Frenzied finance movements are rattling domestic economies. Mass migration is engendering fear and uncertainty. Overlaying everything our digitizing world and its disruptive technologies is providing both vast opportunities and significant threats.

This massive, urgent task requires bureaucracies that have imaginative incentives and regulatory regimes; new methods of internal working that help bring out the best in people; and new relationships with its citizens. These are the three pillars of a more creative bureaucracy.

There is an immense literature on the attempts to address the systemic problems of bureaucratic effectiveness or innovations in governance,

---

1 https://en.creativebureaucracy.net/.

both in public and in private organizations. This literature on reform has grown exponentially. Yet we have discovered none that looks at the issues from the perspective of the individual bureaucrat and their human potential. Instead, too much discussion is on how to rethink processes as we adjust and seek to maximize the potential of the digital world. Innovation always seems to mean technology.

A change in focus was essential. There are vast numbers of people who feel that working for the public interest is a vocation, but if the image of bureaucracies is negative it will not attract the younger people it needs to replenish the organization. The challenge of the era is to find ways to mobilize human potential. So here is a dilemma. The bureaucracy can systematically reduce the quality of its talent. *It recruits many of the brightest. It trains them to conform.* It creates rule followers. The more independently minded leave as most individuals have an inner impulse to express themselves.

The public administration cannot address future wicked problems without talent, unless it, with its stakeholders, sees itself as a 'community of brains'. Then a different paradigm and value set emerges. The more open bureaucracy helps this process.

There is a reservoir of hidden potential and talent locked up in public bureaucracies. People can do much more if given the chance. This can unleash their discretionary effort, the desire to do more than you need to. But hard-wired, rigid approaches within and across administrative systems, organizations and individuals constrain what is possible.

Every individual has a vast storehouse of 'discretionary' effort that they daily either give or withhold. Discretionary effort is the difference between how well people are capable of performing and how well they actually perform. It is both in the power of employees and a factor of systems that can encourage or prevent people from making contributions. Once people are at work with their full selves, creative potential can emerge.

Frightening statistics tell a story about disengagement and under achievement at work. Our surveys show that on average people work at only 65 per cent capacity. They tell us they could do 35 per cent more if their operating environment were different. Good managers, leaders and committed staff overwork themselves, operating at 120 per cent capacity. Adobe's global benchmark study[2] of 5000 adults across the world explored attitudes and beliefs about creativity at work, school and home. Over 80 per cent agreed that 'unlocking creative potential is key to economic and societal growth'. Yet 'less than half describe themselves as creative'. Only one in four people feel they are living up to their creative potential at work, especially given the increasing pressure to be productive rather than creative at work.

Levels of frustration are growing as *bureaucracies have more highly educated employees than ever before.* These employees are no longer content to be voiceless, to be infantilized or to be treated as less intelligent or capable than they are. They are irritated that people think only the outsiders have clarity and clever ideas. They want to bring the sense of freedom and autonomy associated with start-up cultures to their day-to-day bureaucratic work. Public sector cultures which emphasize process, hierarchies or levels are rife with internal competition and therefore increasingly less attractive to the most ambitious.

Bureaucrats know there are other ways to work out there. Their experiences in social networks and passion-driven activities are more informal and adaptive. There they contribute within a community of equals. Technology helps create the exchange platforms that drive the necessary sharing. And the web 3.0, based on a world of sensorized objects, with its immersive, ever-present interactive capabilities and use of artificial intelligence, is set to change communication even more dramatically.

Bureaucracies need to help people feel this sense of freedom. The regularity, reliability and accountability of the bureaucratic form needs to meet the 'fleet of foot' of the digitally enabled world. They need to become empathetic environments that trigger a positive psychological response to bring out the best in people.

People know there are ways of communicating without stressing 'who's in charge'. This challenges too traditional notions of democracy. The combination of principle and technology has made working transparently with more shared control possible. The communications

---

2 *State to Create Study: Global Benchmark Study on Attitudes and Beliefs about Creativity at Work, School and Home,* https://www.adobe.com/aboutadobe/pressroom/pdfs/Adobe_State_of_Create_Global_Benchmark_Study.pdf.

revolution has broken the monopoly of the public sector. This may be a blessing.

In the past, restrictive attitudes were often etched into how codes were written. Risk aversion trumps imaginative thinking – mostly. It led to an attitude that 'everything is forbidden unless it is allowed' rather than 'everything is allowed unless it is forbidden'. It is easier to say 'no' when regulations entwine at cross-purposes. Risk-averse interpretation can neutralize good intentions. There is less the courage to say 'yes'.

Bureaucrats often have strong principles, great intentions and good ideas. Most want to do good. Yet we are not naïve to the complexities of working lives in organizations. There are 'pen pushers' as in commercial organizations. But is the individual at fault or dysfunctional organizations or systems? Humane systems bring out people's better selves.

What is required to entice individuals to give this extra effort? It is a mix of both general and specific things: a positive, respectful atmosphere; an ethos that sharing and helping out is good and it will be reciprocated; creating excitement about a project, a target or a goal; making people feel they have agency; stressing how everyone counts and that your contribution matters and has an impact; ensuring you are identified with the outcome and praised; providing an incentive, a reward or a personal gain; perhaps personalizing a challenge to inspire. In addition, it involves creating a culture where slacking and task avoiding feels wrong. An emotionally strong organization will seek to understand the motivations of those that slack and try to get them to switch so they might contribute to the team. Slackers deflate an organization.

This goes beyond simplistic notions around management systems. Fundamental is an attitude of leadership that sees the organization as a joint endeavour where everyone is essential and where everyone can learn and teach. This requires systems that allow rather than curtail, and that create a dynamic which leverages strengths. Most studies say this involves widespread leadership rather than management. Systems are managed; people are led. Everyone can play a leadership role. Here leadership is defined as a relationship rather than a position, so it is behaviour-based. Self-awareness and empathy are key components in the relationship's success.

In fact the best work often happens in a spirit of play, but most organizations expect people to be serious. It's inevitable that work elicits our full range of emotions. But employees are expected to operate almost without emotion, as if 'the system' were a lifeless being.

Startling, under-explored facts about the alienation and distress people feel are largely missing in global discussions of innovation, especially that related to the public sector. Working within a 'system' can feel qualitatively different to working in, say, a start-up. A system can feel pervasive. You see it in worn-down, drained faces of people who have been 'in the system' too long. They are going through the motions. But others refuse to surrender. They rebel. They count victories in small advances.

Qualities of inventiveness are less embedded, legitimized or encouraged in public entities. Yet these energies spill over and burst out. Imagination sometimes is expressed in convoluted ways to make an impact. In essence *bureaucratic creativity is about finding solutions* by overcoming obstacles to intractable problems or discovering fresh opportunities. My book *The Creative City* highlighted the urgency of civic creativity. It said:

> 'Civic creativity' is defined as imaginative problem-solving applied to public good objectives. The aim is to generate a continual flow of innovative solutions to problems which have an impact on the public realm. 'Civic creativity' is the capacity for public officials and others oriented to the public good to effectively and instrumentally apply their imaginative faculties. (Landry 2000)

The imaginative bureaucrat is the (often) invisible guide behind civic creativity. Their efforts, in combination, result in this new value-driven organizational form, and they are adaptive, responsive, flexible, collaborative and outward-looking. They encourage others in executing tasks that inevitably can be routine, yet also inventive. They connect people at a humane level at work and create the conditions needed for openness and creativity to emerge. If they are sufficiently influential they transform their organizations, which embody their values.

Instead, public administrations across the world have not been able to resist the rise of the new managerialism. The resulting efficiency paradigms have partly been beneficial in reshaping how bureaucracies operate. They have become more accountable to their publics. But there are negatives. *One consequence is the overweening box-ticking or checking mentality.* Another is technology being projected as the saviour, with the proliferation of automated systems that feel robotic, or decisions made by algorithms that fail the test for common sense, with services unable to respond to individual circumstances.

Managerialism ceaselessly pushes an approach whereby all human affairs are driven by instrumental rationality, and this can constrain being experimental and trying things out. The most cost-effective means to achieve things always trumps other values or ethical bases. The economic value lens is now the overarching narrative of our world. Something valuable is lost in making citizens become customers. To be identified merely as a customer is a narrow conception of being human.

The intrinsic value of the 'public sector model' itself thus suffered. Instead of upgrading the public service we tried to make it conform to a private sector model; management consultants, essentially accountants, were brought in. They imposed their own discipline – targets and new public management. The possibility of the public sector embracing its own kind of entrepreneurial spirit akin to that of the private sector was lost.

More recently a series of public innovation agencies have been set up. One of the first was Mindlab in Denmark, which existed from 2002 to 2018 and has now been superseded both by a 'Disruption Taskforce'[3] focused more narrowly on digital and technological transformation and by the National Centre for Public Sector Innovation[4] whose innovation barometer is impressive. There is also the Office of Public Sector Innovation (OPSI)[5] in the Organisation for Economic Co-operation and Development (OECD), which is monitoring bureaucratic innovations in its member countries.

Our challenge is that we are in the midst of redesigning the world and all its systems for 21st-century conditions. Its principles should be *to bend the market to bigger-picture purposes.* This needs a bureaucracy that can draw on all its ethical, creative and intellectual resources and reclaim a distinctive leadership role but framed in a 21st-century

---

3 https://em.dk/ministeriet/organisation/departementets-organisation/disruption-taskforce/.

4 https://www.coi.dk/en/.

5 https://oecd-opsi.org/.

context. This organization can have a simple mantra to move from a *'no, because culture'* to a *'yes, if culture'*.

References

Landry, Charles (2000), *The Creative City: A Toolkit for Urban Innovators*, London: Earthscan.

Landry, Charles and Margie Caust (2017), *The Creative Bureaucracy and Its Radical Common Sense*, Stroud, UK: Comedia.

16 Measuring the pulse of places

The aim of the creative cities agenda is for cities to become human centred with associated rights and responsibilities. It involves harnessing people's potential, providing them with a sense of well-being and helping them to become more prosperous and resilient. To do this involves making the most of assets, and what is considered an asset broadens dramatically. Normally cities have thought of assets as tangible, such as a transport system, a research institute, an iconic building, or a large firm. Increasingly, less definable assets are seen as important. They include 'being creative', 'having talent', 'being socially inclusive', 'civic pride', or the 'atmosphere' of a place or 'eco-awareness', and other non-material things like 'urban reputation' or a city's 'resonance'.

The balance sheet of a city can involve the:

- Hard, material and tangible or soft, immaterial and intangible.
- Real and visible or symbolic and invisible.
- Countable, quantifiable and calculable or subjective, qualitative and intuitive.

Clearly the major resource in any city is its people and the way in which they are acknowledged and can express themselves fully. Then there is/are:

- The natural setting: the weather, the seasons, the topography, water, trees, hills and what humans have made from them like parks, lakes or experiences.
- Natural resources: forests, landscapes and those in the ground.
- History, heritage and tradition: in the built fabric, in memories and rituals, in acquired skills.
- The built fabric: the quality of overall design, the pattern of streets and neighbourhoods, the balance between good ordinary buildings, the spectacular and iconic and representative structures.

- Infrastructure: the qualities of information technology, connectivity, train and metro services, roads and streets, sewage systems, power supplies, housing and office stock.
- Urban housekeeping: noise maintenance, rubbish collection and social care.
- Industries: embedded skills in older industries that have been re-engineered to new economy capabilities, the presence of emerging, cutting-edge sectors.
- Services: the sophistication and reach of business-to-business services from finance to law, the reputation of the hospitality industry.
- Skills and talent: educational achievements and choice at different levels, research institutes, informal training possibilities.
- Retailing: the depth and range of shopping choices, from the mainstream to independents to alternative shops.
- Commercial showcasing: conferencing or trade fairs.
- Recreational activities: both involving direct participation and being entertained, such as sports, the arts, museums or galleries, community-based activities, festivals and events.
- Gastronomy: the diversity of food experiences and ratings of restaurants.
- Third spaces: the range and quality of cafés, public gathering and meeting places.
- Investability: the regulations and incentives regime, the right balance of price points from the cheap to the exclusively expensive in relation to housing, commercial development or general investment opportunities.
- Safety and security: low levels of crime, trustworthy institutions, overall reliability.
- Attitudes and attributes: a culture of curiosity, openness, tolerance, joined-up thinking, a 'can do' approach, or entrepreneurship.
- Perceptions: clarity of recognition and reputation, a sense of vibrancy.
- Governance, organization, management and delivery: traditions of 'walking the talk', empowering the workforce, strong partnership working.

Auditing obstacles is just as important as auditing assets. The major challenge often is to use imagination to turn an obstacle, such as difficult weather, into an asset, or to identify something that can become unique or special for a city. An urban obstacle, by contrast, is when a potential is underdeveloped or when there is a bigger context over which a place has no control. Many cities are doing well economically but may well be socially divided, and their quality of life may be suffering. This provides opportunities for others, especially secondary cities and the many cities that are shrinking. It is with these, those increasingly left behind, that we need to use our inventiveness and skill.

Classic definitions of urban success

The shifts described in this book change how we measure the success of a city or region. Classically the attributes assessed were:

- Location
- Physical characteristics
- Infrastructure
- Human resources
- Finance and capital
- Knowledge and technology
- Industrial structure
- Institutional capacity
- Business culture.

A more modern way of describing assets that evolved in the 1990s is:

- Economic profile
- Market prospects
- Tax levels
- Regulatory framework
- Labour climate
- Suppliers and know-how
- Utilities
- Incentives
- Quality of life
- Logistics
- Sites
- Community identity and image.

Another way of describing urban potential has been the concept of drawing power.[1] This assesses the dynamics of attraction and retention as well as its reverse – leakage and what deters or even repels people

---

1 Developed by Charles Landry, initially with Franco Bianchini, in various publications from 2000 onwards.

from cities. It is a multidimensional concept. It combines an assessment of both hard and soft factors giving more equal weighting to both, and it judges each factor and asset in economic, social, cultural and environmental terms. Drawing power looks at the city from the inside and outside, through both calculable realities and perceptions. Its assessment criteria are:

- Critical mass
- Identity and distinctiveness
- Innovative capacity
- Diversity, accessibility
- Security and safety
- Linkage and synergy
- Competitiveness
- Organizational capacity
- Leadership.

Each of these elements in turn is judged holistically. Take diversity as an instance. The diversity of the economic structure usually increases local resilience. Harnessing the diversity in the population can make a strong contribution to urban success economically, culturally and socially. The diversity of the urban setting helps create richer experiences and the cultural diversity is seen as an expression of cosmopolitanism.

Alternatively, take critical mass. Critical mass is concerned with the achievement of appropriate thresholds to allow activity to take off, reinforce itself and cluster. Economically it involves the agglomeration of sufficient activities to ensure that economies of scale, inter-firm cooperation and synergies are obtained. It represents the thresholds beyond which the organization of particular economic initiatives such as trade fairs, foreign trade missions, promotion and inward investment campaigns become possible. Socially, critical mass could be identified as the density of social interactions. Physically, critical mass assesses the sheer mass, say, of historic buildings sufficient to form an attractive and marketable heritage quarter. Culturally, critical mass is the opportunity of experiencing different types of facilities, such as going in the course of the same evening to a French bistro, a pop-up play and a late-night cabaret in a wine bar, and then enjoying a stroll through a pleasant historic area.

Innovative capacity implies looking at all kinds of innovations to make a city work, such as social innovations like providing local services through a voluntary group or cultural innovations like using social media which speeds up interaction. Security as a concept is not only about physical safety, but also the stability of employment or the feeling that being culturally anchored has a value.

A city's overall drawing power needs to take into account how the different spatial areas – including the city centre, the inner city areas surrounding it, the residential suburbs, the outer residential and industrial areas, and the edge of town – operate as an interconnected competitive system. Each part of a city has its specific level of drawing power.

There is an even crisper summary of the overall themes to describe the urban assets fostered by 'CEOs for Cities' in its publication *City Vitals*.[2] It involves assessing:

- Talent
- Connections
- Innovation
- Distinctiveness.

Ranking systems

The many systems that attempt to rank the major cities of the world in terms of their urban competitiveness or the reputation of their learning systems include the following: Mercer Consulting Group, the Economist Intelligence Unit, the IMD, the Globalisation and World Cities Study Group, Global Liveable Cities Index, the Jones Lang Lasalle's Winning Cities Programme, Richard Florida's Creativity Index, the Times Higher Educational Supplement, Shanghai Jiao Tong University Ranking, University Webometrics, Monocle and 2thinknow.

The '2thinknow' *Innovation* Cities™ *Index, for instance, started in 2006, and looks at three key factors: networked markets, which assesses a city's power and linkages in global markets; human infrastructure, which includes the soft and hard issues of mass transit and roads, finance, law, healthcare, telecommunications and universities; and cultural assets, measured by a city's arts communities, civic organizations, museums,*

2 https://ceosforcities.org/portfolio/city-vitals-30/.

music events, media and even political protests.[3] *Beyond that it looks at 35 sectors with 160 plus indicators.*

Ranking cities has become a new fashion. There is wide variation in the rankings attributed to different cities, as each ranking system tends to adopt a different set of indicators for assessment: some are focused around a city's economic performance or global connectivity, while others seek to assess city performance from a liveability, quality-of-life or 'innovation' perspective.

While there is no universally agreed hierarchy that emerges from these rankings, there is some consensus around the 40 or so globally connected cities that always come up. This leaves the thousands of potentially interesting smaller unrecognized cities.

Rankings and league tables themselves have become competitive tools. They clearly assess a city, but they are also marketing tools. For instance, Singapore has created the Centre for Liveable Cities and comes high on its own rankings. Crucially ranking systems have to be looked at with caution. Monocle has had one of the most fine-grained and interesting quality-of-life indices, but what is noticeable is that since the Japanese company Nikkei bought a stake in 2014 Japanese cities like Tokyo and Fukuoka have tended to score very highly – perhaps deserved. Commentators have asked 'Is Tokyo really the best city in the world?', after it topped the survey three times from 2015 to 2017.

A core question too is 'who is commissioning and organizing the study?' Mercers, for instance, is a human resources and related financial advice organization, and so has a particular perspective. Interestingly Calgary was once nominated the top eco-city in Mercers scorecard. This simply beggars belief when renowned eco-cities like Stockholm and Copenhagen were joint 9th and Hamburg 35th, which questions the whole ranking system. Either there are different conceptions of what sustainability means in North America in contrast to Europe, or the assessment criteria are inadequate. Mercers assesses water availability and drinkability, waste removal, quality of sewage systems, air pollution and traffic congestion, which is a very narrow conception of sustainability. Yet the marketing value of being able to say 'the world's number one eco-city' is immense. Another example of possible bias is

---

3 https://www.innovation-cities.com/city-rankings/.

in the Economist Intelligence Unit rankings, where English-speaking cities have a disproportionate number of entries – six in the top ten in 2018.

There are inadequate criteria in global university rankings. In part this is because of their Anglo-American bias and, in terms of education, the bias towards rating PhDs, and then largely in the natural sciences and primary research. By contrast, many of the innovations emerging are coming from the social sciences and humanities, or from design-oriented or more artistic disciplines, where very few PhDs are written. As one vice chancellor noted: 'The best way to get up the rankings is to get rid of the arts.'

Measuring creativity

There is a vast literature on creativity, and it has been assessed from the perspective of many academic fields. Areas covered include what creativity is, its history, biographies of creative individuals (mostly scientists and artists), the processes involved in generating creative ideas, techniques of measuring and assessing degrees of creativity, and methods of encouraging people to be more creative and how you measure it. This literature is overwhelmingly focused on individuals and whether and how they are creative. Interest in creativity in organizations is now growing substantially, and over the last two decades the idea of creative cities and regions has moved up the agenda.

Measuring individual creativity

There are many tests to measure individual creativity, perhaps two hundred. Too many look at artistic capacities. In essence they highlight a few things: patterns of thought can change, ideas can be liberated through tools, and new solutions can be found. There are techniques to increase the number of ideas, to generate new ideas and reframe old ones. They rely on opening out and switching perspective, shifting the mindset or bringing complex ideas together.

Measuring the creativity of organizations

People now ask what makes creative organizations. First this involved removing blocks to individual creativity, such as allowing music, making work more fun and forcing mental breaks in the work routine, or running team-building exercises, establishing work schedules and changing work environments in order to inspire and to generate passion. Simultaneously attempts were made to develop a culture and context where there is freedom to act, where the right level of challenge is set up and creativity is rewarded in performance evaluation. Finally, awareness grew that the inside and outside of the workplace is important. Ultimately the qualities of the urban environment and their amenities have become significant.

Measuring the creativity of cities and regions

There is an extensive history of research on regional innovation as well as some on creative milieux. This research focuses on issues like research capacity and the reputation of universities, clustering, and the availability of venture capital and infrastructure support. Gunnar Törnqvist and Åke Andersson were associated with developing this concept in the early to mid-1980s. This debate received a new push through the work of Richard Florida. A central message of his work is that whereas in the past people moved to jobs, now jobs move to people. This means that cities and regions need a people climate as well as a jobs climate. Those places, Florida claims, that are attractive are the ones that will lure the 'creative class' – those employed in coming up with new ideas and better ways of doing things, which includes knowledge nomads, the research community and those involved in the creative economy. These are places with strong amenity and creativity. Yet that ground is shifting. Comedia's own Creative Cities Index looks at places in terms of how they identify and nurture all talents, how empowering a place is, how the talent identified is enabled and encouraged by the political regime, what is done to harness and exploit that potential and, finally, whether the lived experience of the place generates an open and generous atmosphere.

Measuring the creativity of a system

Measuring creativity ecosystems, especially across countries, is in its infancy. Yet there is a vast range of organizations, from the OECD to the EU, with its European Innovation Scoreboard (EIS), to universities and private sector institutions, assessing the measurement of innovation and innovation systems. The annual EIS provides a comparative assessment of research and innovation performance and the relative strengths and weaknesses of national research and innovation systems across the 28 EU countries and 20 others.[4] However, the EIS is limited to looking at companies, investments and economic framework indicators rather than having a wider scope.

One important study was by Hugo Hollanders and Adriana van Cruysen, who prepared a report in 2009 for the European Commission titled *Design, Creativity and Innovation: A Scoreboard Approach*.[5] It was one of the first attempts to measure creativity across a system and cross-nationally. It revealed a strong correlation between creativity, design and innovation. They acknowledge that measuring creativity and design in quantitative and statistical terms, and its contribution at regional, national and international levels, is a problem given the lack of indicators and data. The route Hollanders and Cruysen took was to use three proxy indicators or indirect measures: creative education, self-expression, and openness and tolerance. The best performing countries in relation to creativity and design are the innovation leaders, and these are Finland, Sweden, Germany and Denmark.

Dilemmas in measuring cities

The key issues in measuring cities are the nature of the available data; the relative importance of subjective and objective, quantitative and qualitative data; how data can be compared between cities; the proportion and extent of a given attribute being measured; the specificity of the local context; and, finally, how data is weighted.

There is a vast amount of data about the economic and social conditions of countries and regions, and it is possible to use this broad-based core information generated from national statistical offices to make national comparisons.

Inevitably this data is very general, such as how many people live in an area, birth or death rates, or the number of business start-ups or of cars. There are not as yet long-term statistics at the city level internationally that help us understand the precise dynamics of a city. Furthermore, it is difficult to compare information that is regionally or locally collected, perhaps for a specific study, and that is not nationally collated,

---

4 file:///C:/Users/charl/Downloads/MEMO-17-1674_EN.pdf.

5 http://digitalarchive.maastrichtuniversity.nl/fedora/get/guid%3Aea137e86-d8ad-41dd-b0ac-a04 65d0d4161/ASSET1/.

or information that is deemed to be confidential and is not readily available, such as some crime data. The same holds true for information collected on environmental questions such as air pollution, noise, soil contamination and water quality, which are often not gathered, although it is getting better.

To assess a city properly you need a combination of subjective and objective data. Furthermore, how good a city is depends on a mix of reality and truth, hype, image and perception, usually filtered through media representations. Data thus needs to be looked at in four different ways:

- Subjective measures of subjective phenomena – for example, how safe do people feel?
- Objective measures of subjective phenomena – for example, how much do people spend weekly on taxis because they are afraid of walking home at night?
- Subjective measures of objective phenomena – for example, to what extent are people satisfied with lighting in the neighbourhood or the frequency of public transport?
- Objective measures of objective phenomena – for example, how frequent is the bus service or how many events has the arts centre put on?

Objective data can be quantified and measured, while subjective data can only be assessed and judged. In looking at something as complex as a city, it is unlikely that a simple set of quantitative data will provide an accurate picture. It is always necessary to read this data in the light of local conditions and to understand the correlations between types of data. For example, there is a correlation between background demographic data and data on the usage of the city centre in the evening by a particular social group.

It is possible to establish a core set of indicators against which the performance of a city can regularly be monitored through quantified data such as how well its retailing is doing. This, however, is not sufficient. In addition, it is necessary to establish a methodology for garnering qualitative background information through which the significance of changes in the performance of a city can be adequately judged. For example, civic pride is an important ingredient for the viability of a city. To an extent this can be measured by proxy data such as the levels of readership, the audiences for local papers, radio or other local media, or levels of volunteerism and the number of NGOs, but this will not be adequate to make a thorough assessment of civic pride. More questions within general categories such as the presence of civic societies will have to be asked. It may also be necessary to ask more detailed questions about local traditions, rituals and other aspects of local history.

In summary, quantitative data are important because they tell you what exists. However, they have to be complemented by qualitative data, which are suitable for explaining why and how something exists and how it changes over time.

Each positive attribute carries with it potential negative side effects. For instance, diversity as a broad concept is seen as good, such as a wide network of firms, but too much diversity may become a negative feature, such as when too many incomers arrive in a city at great speed, which can overwhelm a city even though the diversity dividend is important. Accessibility similarly is seen as positive; but on the other hand, if places such as a recreation facility become too popular, it can turn into a negative. The same is true for cities: too much popularity can destroy the local quality of life.

The key concept here is *threshold* – when does a good attribute turn into a bad one? There are thus benchmarks, although they are difficult to identify for all circumstances.

In terms of specific local context, the question is not only about how much of something exists, say car parking, but also where it is located. Superficially it may appear that, say, a city centre has adequate parking in comparison with competitor cities. However, the car parks may be located in the wrong place and thus do not contribute to the viability of the city centre because they are slightly off centre and regarded by shoppers as too inconvenient.

Finally, how do you weigh what is important? According to conventional wisdom, economic issues are generally perceived to be the most important. However, available surveys suggest that in some cities people give a higher importance to non-economic issues such as the social connections, the quality of the environment or its history. Therefore, what is deemed to be important is in part a political issue.

The Creative City Index[6]

The Creative City Index (Landry and Hyams 2012) assesses ten cross-cutting domains, themselves devised by drawing in knowledge about the success and failure of cities. These are clustered within four groupings which describe the creative ecology and dynamics of a place. The Index looks at places holistically from the economic, cultural and social points of view, as well as assesses the deeper shifts and trends happening either technologically, in terms of environmental needs, or politically, that affect our urban futures. It needs to take into account global agendas such as the SDG debates.

The aim is to provide an assessment framework, the results of which can be used to create urban strategies and generate specific recommendations. A strategic conversation is always proposed that emerges from interpreting the results, which combine a subjective self-assessment with an external view. The differences between these two perspectives have so far had the greatest impact on the nearly 25 cities which have participated in working with the Index. These include Bilbao, Helsinki, Oulu, Gijon, Ghent, Antwerp, Mannheim and Crakow in Europe, and Taipei and Adelaide elsewhere. The momentum generated can be catalytic and transformative.

Internal and external assessment

The Creative City Index is different from other evaluation exercises because of the internal and subjective and the external and more objective assessment. To get a deeper view takes time and background research on the city. Then an extensive programme of visits is necessary to experience the city and its lived life first-hand. This involves seeing facilities, institutions, companies and organizations before, as in any research initiative, a wide-ranging series of one-to-one and group interviews with knowledgeable and credible people across a diversity of sectors is undertaken, where interviewees individually and collectively assess how well their city is doing. At the same time, but separately, web-based questionnaires are completed to capture a far-wider audience. All these activities resolve to a score based on weighting devices and a series of analytical tools.

The differences between the internal and external evaluations are critical as both the gap and the overall score given provide the basis for

---

6 See https://charleslandry.com/themes/creative-cities-index/.

assessing weaknesses and strengths and the means for evaluating how to move forward. In addition, the Index provides the ability to compare and contrast with all other participating cities, who can share information.

Indicators of a creative place

The urban dynamics are distilled into four clusters comprising ten domains, or groups of indicators for creativity. Within each of these there are key traits or questions indicating creativity. The four clusters assess how the city:

Nurtures and identifies its creative potential
  1. Openness, trust, tolerance and accessibility
  2. Talent and learning landscape

Enables and supports creative capacity to maximize prospects
  3. Political and public framework
  4. Strategic leadership, agility and vision
  5. Professionalism and effectiveness

Exploits and harnesses its expertise, talents and aspirations
  6. Entrepreneurship, exploration and innovation
  7. Communication, connectivity and networking

Expresses this in the lived experience of the city
  8. Distinctiveness, diversity, vitality and expression
  9. The place and place-making
  10. Liveability and well-being

The qualities measured

A higher score within the four clusters and ten domain headings requires a strong showing in the following qualities: motivation, tenacity, awareness, clarity of communication, broad thinking, inspiration, aspiration, adaptability, dynamism, openness, participation, design awareness, sensory appreciation, professional pride and technical competence, leadership, or vision.

Areas explored

The audit looks at the culture of a place, broadly defined, and the extent to which it is acting according to the best of its imaginative possibilities across the spectrum from the individual, to the firm, to industry sectors and clusters, to social organizations, to networks in the city, to the city itself as an amalgam of different organizational cultures, and to the region. It needs to assess the relevance of creativity in the community and in the private and public sectors as well as in relation to the arts and cultural scene, areas like education and science, and specific industry sectors and businesses, in helping the prosperity and well-being of the region. This helps us to understand the dynamics of a place.

In relation to the private sector, while it assesses the culture of industry and the creativity of the new economy, such as in the creative industries, it also reviews the creativity potential of traditional industries. For instance, some aspects of ship building are both advanced and traditional, as could also be the case in a field like ceramics.

A second area of investigation is social entrepreneurship and the culture of self-help and self-organizing – often a means of empowering people in local communities to take responsibility and to develop entrepreneurship and solve social problems at the same time.

A third is exploring the creativity of public sector organizations in both delivering services and enabling their communities to flourish. This looks at 'civic creativity', defined as imaginative problem solving applied to public good objectives. 'Civic creativity' is the capacity for public officials and others oriented to public good aims to effectively and instrumentally apply their imaginative faculties to achieving 'higher value within a framework of social and political values' (Landry 2000). A key question is how creativity and its intrinsic need for flexibility can be married to strong accountability principles. It explores cross-disciplinary working. This is part of the creative bureaucracy agenda.

In a fourth area, levels of creativity are evaluated in working across sectors and interorganizational networking. This seeks to explore the extent to which value-added is created through inventive partnering and networking, for instance between business, universities and social groups, or the relationship of business to arts and cultural development.

A fifth area of focus is boundary-busting creativity. For example, from the beginning of the 21st century a rapprochement has begun between the two great ways of exploring, understanding and knowing: science, technology and art. This collaborative activity has generated considerable momentum and become a powerful force for change and innovation in the development of new products, processes and services. To what extent are there projects that combine the artistic with the technological, or apply more artistic approaches to planning, or bring the artistic community into the urban planning arena?

A sixth area of exploration is assessing how the conditions for creativity are created. This focuses especially on programmes in education and learning. Yet this is not to be restricted to schools and institutions of higher learning, but needs to encompass professional development and other forms of learning also.

A seventh area is an audit of obstacles in generating impact and creativity, as it is increasingly recognized that highlighting obstacles, which themselves become targets for creative action, is at least as important as highlighting best practices. This seeks to address one of today's greatest paradoxes: the rise of the creativity agenda and simultaneous rise of an increased culture of risk aversion.

The final area of the audit looks at how the physical context can support the development of a strong urban creative culture in order to encourage people to stay or be attracted to the city. Overall this audit tells us where a place is and where it could get to by taking into account comparative knowledge of cities elsewhere.

The areas explored include the educational sector, such as university institutions, those responsible for the school curriculum or interesting schools. The public administration is also examined, including departments such as urban planning, transport, economic development, the health service, the environment, social affairs, culture and education, as these affect how the city develops.

Within business it is important to discuss innovative capacity with both high-tech companies and companies operating in traditional spheres and advanced manufacturing, as creativity is not limited to the former. That capacity includes too innovation centres, high-tech parks and incubator units. Within services there are three main categories to be explored: the cultural and creative economy, including design, the new media, music and related sectors as well as cultural institutions such as galleries and the performance sectors; tourism and hospitality, including agents, hoteliers and restaurants; and business-to-business services, such as finance, insurance and accountancy as well as consultancy.

In the social domain a variety of organizations are explored, including those operating as social entrepreneurs as well as social help or activist bodies. The media play a significant role in both generating identity and projecting a city. They are often negative about their city and need to be brought in.

Finally, in any city there is a group of interesting and influential people who do not fit into any special category but are important for reading the capacities and potential of a place. In various stages of the evaluation, groupings from different domains are mixed.

Catalytic ideas

Finally, measuring and ranking places is ultimately about moving on and doing something, such as dealing with problems and grasping opportunities. Looking at urban assets and the complexity of cities, it is important to ask 'what is a good, catalytic idea or programme or strategy that can drive a process, that becomes the roadmap to move forward?' A great idea needs to trigger and drive ambition. It needs to be simple but complex in its potential. A good idea is instantly understandable, resonates and communicates iconically – you grasp it in one. A good idea needs to have layers and depth, and be able to be interpreted and expressed creatively in many ways as well as involve many people who each feel they have something to offer. A good idea connects and suggests linkages. It is dynamic. It breathes and implies multiple possibilities. With a good idea creativity and practicality come together. A good idea solves economic problems as well as others. It also embodies issues beyond the economic. If it is just economic it can become mechanistic. Ideally it should touch the identity of a place and so feel socially and culturally relevant. Indeed, it should support, build on and create this identity. In this way it should speak to deeper values and ambitions. If a catalytic idea is significantly powerful it can be implemented in many ways.

Let's look at some ideas. Many cities around the world say they are going to become the 'education city'. This idea is narrow; it implies and feels as if it is only the education sector that is involved. It excludes everyone else. 'A talent strategy for . . .' idea would be better; it is easy to understand, and clearly many people would need to be engaged; participants from many sectors can foresee their involvement: from the arts to education, to business providing professional development. It can be layered to focus on identifying, harnessing, attracting, sustaining or exploiting talent, or it can focus on the stages of talent, from getting people to be curious and then to becoming enterprising, entrepreneurial or innovative. Its weakness is that it could apply anywhere. To say, as Memphis once said, that it is 'The City of Second Chances' is quite strong. It projects a positive ethos: openness, the willingness to listen, tolerance. It recognizes that the city is disadvantaged without exaggerating. It acknowledges business start-up records are not too good. It opens out to the future and ideally in a decade the slogan will be less relevant, because enough second chancers will have succeeded. To say that Adelaide would 'waterproof the city' was a strong idea of theirs, but it unfortunately never happened. It had an implied economic agenda and spoke powerfully to green issues. The same could be true if any other city were to claim it would become the world's first 'zero emissions city' or 'solar city', and really mean it. Copenhagen's target is 2025, Helsinki's 2035 and Stockholm's 2040, and Masdar in the United Arab Emirates (UAE) is attempting to grow its city in a carbon-neutral way. It would provide a mass of business opportunities and put any city on the global radar screen. It would be interesting and counter-intuitive for a known mining centre or industrial centre to try to be carbon neutral.

The central question for a city is 'what good ideas are needed now?' Rather than conventional new technology advances that dominate discussions of innovation, it may be social innovations or projects that help us change our behaviours that are far more important.

To summarize: all places are special in their own way, and when they work well one can imagine them being able to create the ultimate mix, which is becoming:

- A place of distinctiveness and anchorage. Somewhere that feels like home, that generates a sense of the known and comforting. A place that celebrates where it comes from but is confident in where it is going.
- A place of connection and reconnection. Somewhere that is locally bonded yet at ease with the global, and that has seamless connectivity from the physical to the virtual.

- A place of possibility. Somewhere that is open-minded and encourages curiosity, and which provides choices and opportunities in differing phases of life.
- A place of learning. Somewhere with many possibilities to self-improve, from the formal to the informal; a place where a discussion culture is vibrant and things are thought about afresh.
- A place of inspiration. Somewhere with a visionary feel, where aspiration and good intent is made visible in interesting ways and therefore create a positive virtual spiral.
- A place of adding values and value simultaneously in any major initiative it undertakes. Somewhere where economic drive is framed by an ethical value base.

References

Landry, Charles (2000), *The Creative City: A Toolkit for Urban Innovators*, London: Earthscan.

Landry, Charles and Jonathan Hyams (2012), *The Creative City Index: Measuring the Pulse of Your City*, Stroud, UK: Comedia.

Acknowledgements

You cannot write a book without being influenced by others and I have been helped and inspired by many friends, collaborators and authors. They include Franco Bianchini, Phil Wood, Jonathan Hyams, Margie Caust, Richard Brecknock, Chris Murray, Carol Coletta, Sir Peter Hall, Klaus Kunzmann, Timo Cantell, Bill McAlister, Marc Pachter, Tom Burke, Rodin Genoff, Lynda Dorrington, Rainer Kern, Margaret Shiu, Hamdan Majeed, Francois Matarasso, Do-in Choi, Lia Ghilardi, Sebastian Turner, Masayuki Sasaki, Idoia Postigo, Lyndsay Neilsen, Fredrik Lindegren, Liesbeth Jansen, Peter Kageyama, Bob Palmer, Ken Worpole, Cornelia Dümcke, Veronika Ratzenböck, Vera Boltho, Jose Manuel Diogo, Duarte de Lima Mayer, Gabriella Gomez Mont, Christian Hübel, Colin Mercer, Stephen Hodes, Carol Steinberg, Avril Joffe, Ana Carla Fonseca, Bernd Fesel, Tim Jones, Marco Raino, Andrea and Florinda Bartoli, Jan Lerch, Ania Pilipenko, Jochen Sandig, Dimitri Hegemann, Robin Schellenberg, Maciej Wojciechowski, Kai Yin Lo, Desmond Hui, Laurence Lo, Pekka Timonen, Harm Christian Tolden, Karl-Filip Coenegrachts and Kim Cook.

Index

Titles in the **Elgar Advanced Introductions** series include:

International Political Economy
Benjamin J. Cohen

The Austrian School of Economics
Randall G. Holcombe

Cultural Economics
Ruth Towse

Law and Development
Michael J. Trebilcock and Mariana Mota Prado

International Humanitarian Law
Robert Kolb

International Trade Law
Michael J. Trebilcock

Post Keynesian Economics
J.E. King

International Intellectual Property
Susy Frankel and Daniel J. Gervais

Public Management and Administration
Christopher Pollitt

Organised Crime
Leslie Holmes

Nationalism
Liah Greenfeld

Social Policy
Daniel Béland and Rianne Mahon

Globalisation
Jonathan Michie

Entrepreneurial Finance
Hans Landström

International Conflict and Security Law
Nigel D. White

Comparative Constitutional Law
Mark Tushnet

International Human Rights Law
Dinah L. Shelton

Entrepreneurship
Robert D. Hisrich

International Tax Law
Reuven S. Avi-Yonah

Public Policy
B. Guy Peters

The Law of International Organizations
Jan Klabbers

International Environmental Law
Ellen Hey

International Sales Law
Clayton P. Gillette

Corporate Venturing
Robert D. Hisrich

Public Choice
Randall G. Holcombe

Private Law
Jan M. Smits

Consumer Behavior Analysis
Gordon Foxall

Behavioral Economics
John F. Tomer

Cost-Benefit Analysis
Robert J. Brent

Environmental Impact Assessment
Angus Morrison-Saunders